# 'Learning to Write, or Writing to Learn?'

*A critical analysis and evaluation of the Schools Council Project of written language of 11- to 18-year-olds and its development project, 'Writing across the Curriculum'*

## Jeanette T. Williams

## NFER Publishing Company Ltd.

*Published by the NFER Publishing Company Ltd.,*
*Darville House, 92-93 Peascod Street,*
*Windsor, Berks. SL4 1DF.*
*Registered Office: The Mere, Upton Park, Slough, Berks. SL1 2DQ*
*First published 1977*
*© Jeanette T. Williams, 1977*
*ISBN 0 85633 128 7*

---

*Typeset by Cameographics Ltd.,*
*63 Milford Road, Reading, Berks.*
*Printed in Great Britain by*
*John Gardner (Printers), Hawthorne Road, Bootle, Merseyside.*
*Distributed in the USA by Humanities Press Inc.,*
*Atlantic Highlands, New Jersey 07716 USA.*

# Contents

# PREFACE

Since *A Language for Life*, the Bullock Report, was published in 1975, concern for the development of language in schools has grown. One of the forms which this concern has taken is the desire to formulate language policies for the whole curriculum, and in consequence, the phrase 'Language across the Curriculum' has become a slogan. This slogan has also given wider currency to the ideas of the Schools Council Project 'Writing across the Curriculum'and its earlier Research Project 'The Development of Writing Abilities 11-18', the authors of which were responsible for its coining.

It seemed to me that these ideas were only half understood, and that they were being implemented with only a very vague idea of their theoretical basis or their implications. In this critique therefore, I first trace the origin and historical development of the Project, to the point where its title first became a slogan. I go on to describe and analyse its main theories and hypotheses about language and learning in order to find out the basis of its claims to be a curriculum development theory. A critical discussion of these theories follows in the third chapter, and the final chapter is an attempt to discuss the role of theory in general in educational research, to relate the Project to different kinds of educational theory, and to evaluate it as *curriculum* research. The conclusion discusses the changing paradigm of curriculum development, and attempts to point the way for future language research in schools.

Introduction

# From Idea to Curriculum Theory: *the evolution of the 'Writing across the Curriculum' Project*

When the first report from the Writing Research Unit set up by the Schools Council to investigate written language in secondary schools, was published in 1975, the sense of *deja vu* was strong, at least among teachers of English. Most of the theories and ideas seemed to have already had a thorough airing elsewhere. This was even more true of the contents of the second document, the report of the developmental part of the project 'Writing and Learning across the Curriculum 11-16', published in Spring 1976.

The theories had indeed been around for a long time. Although published so recently, the Project was set up as long ago as 1966, as part of the initial English programme of the newly-formed Schools Council. A year before, the Council had produced its first policy declarations, and Working Paper Number Three designated English one of three 'top priority areas' proposing a wide-reaching and ambitious programme of research and development. Spurred on by the activities of 'Project English' in America — which it mentioned admiringly — it recommended the setting-up of local English centres to carry out the developmental aspects of the English programme. It plumped decidedly for 'the Universities and Institutes of Education' as the centres of 'long-term research'. A 'Consultative Committee in Communication' was established, which was responsible for initiating and coordinating research into the major aspects of language in schools — speech, comprehension, reading and writing — and most of the members of this were academics or well-known writers on English teaching. Interestingly, the Working Paper reveals an interdisciplinary attitude: 'What constitutes the ability to communicate at various ages for different purposes, and for different social groups?' (p.12). Thus the idea of 'language *across* the curriculum' was born, though not yet christened. For this we had to wait until 1969, with the publication of James Britton's article of that name in Douglas Barnes' *Language, the Learner and the School*.

Meanwhile, a 'proposal to inquire into the development of writing abilities in children aged eleven to eighteen' was drawn up by three members of the London Institute of Education English Department, James Britton, Nancy Martin, and Harold Rosen, and funded for five years as a Schools Council Research Project. (A similar proposal had been mooted earlier, in 1964, to the Nuffield Foundation, but the latter, by a partition agreement with the Council, excluded English work from its field of interest.) Interestingly, it shared priority in the inaugural programme with sixth-form studies, and with surveys and research to prepare schools and teachers for the raising of the school-leaving age from fifteen to sixteen, planned to take effect from 1970. Among the research projects into 'integrated studies', considered to be more suitable for these 'new' pupils than the subject disciplines, was Laurence Stenhouse's 'Humanities Curriculum Project'.

Almost immediately after the Unit was set up, the Dartmouth Conference was convened — the first trans-Atlantic seminar to discuss common problems in English teaching. Many prominent teachers of English, academics, and four members of the 'Consultative Committee' attended from England, including Harold Rosen and James Britton. The English account of what happened at Dartmouth makes it clear that our teachers were less concerned with language development as such, than with those aspects of language which contributed to personal growth and 'self expression' (which emphasis evidently worried the Americans).

This dislike of, and lack of interest in, 'impersonal' language uses in education is evident in the writings of the Writing Research Unit from the beginning, placing them very firmly in the English-teaching ethos of the 60's, which reacted against the 'new technology' and the predominance of science in the post-Sputnik era, and staked everything on an intra — rather than an inter — personal approach. But technology and its 'systems' crept in even here, though perhaps by the back door. Linguistics at this time was a fast-growing field; M.A.K. Halliday had already been working for some time with the Nuffield Foundation (and was shortly to work for the Schools Council) and so had Randolph Quirk. But it was the *ethno-* and *psycho-* linguistics, with its emphasis either on the global or the individual, rather than the *socio-* linguistics of Halliday, which attracted the Writing Research team. A *model* of language-functions was deemed necessary, to replace the verbal description of earlier formulations. The Project had become 'scientific'.

From the start, the 'Writing Research Project' had been closely involved with the fortunes and ideology of the Schools Council, and now began to reflect some of its changes of emphasis. When the Consultative Committee in Communication folded in 1967, only two years after its inauguration, the projects it had sustained under its umbrella drifted apart. Some parts of the ambitious programme were never realized, and those projects which did continue lost their connection with the 'Grand Design', and became inward-looking. In the case of the Writing Research project, this tendency was exacerbated by the fact that all the members of the team were English teachers — although their brief was interdisciplinary — and were for the most part working together in the same Department. (It is this, I think, which accounts for the curiously dated tone of 'The Development of Writing Abilities, 11-18', in terms of what we expect of curriculum research writing of the mid-1970s. It is quite literally of another decade, in conception and overall philosophy.) When the 'research' stage of the Project came to an end in 1971, and the setting-up of a three-year development project was approved, the emphasis was firmly laid on 'investigation in collaboration with teachers in schools of the *practical* application of research'. The Schools Council's policy had changed; no longer was it in favour (nor could it be, given the economic climate and the pressure from all sides on its resources) of large-scale, all-embracing, expensive research projects. The new emphasis was on piecemeal projects with practical outcomes, of more direct use to teachers in the classroom, and which involved them in the research itself. Thus the two publications of the Writing Research Project reflect two distinct stages in the development of the Schools Council's attitude to curriculum research and development, as their remarkably differing styles and presentation suggest.

The first report of the project, soberly entitled 'The Development of Writing Abilities 11-18' is for the most part a modestly written and careful account of the theoretical work of the Team and the conclusions to be drawn from it. The claims for the theory are moderate, and a serious attempt is made to base them on the statistical tables included. (Though if we look for documentation or evidence for the 'development' in the title we shall be disappointed.) The second publication, we can see immediately from the title, has descended from the lofty world of language theory and is attempting to find its place in the cut-and-thrust of the curriculum arena. Inside 'Writing and Learning across the Curriculum 11-16' we find no further development or modification of the theories of the Research project, and no new statistical tables. Nor, however, do we find any analysis of practice. Instead we have an impressionistic account of what (some) children write, in (some) schools, in (some) subjects, an account which proceeds mainly by selected quotation and anecdote. Of course, I am not suggesting that this is what all recently published Schools Council projects are like — merely that the changes mentioned here are the ways in which the Writing Research team has tried to modify its methods in response to the evolving field of curriculum research and development. Its difficulties of accommodation are particularly poignant, I would suggest, because it has been in business for such a long time, and its original ideas which by now must seem to those involved like the tablets handed down on Mount Sinai, need to be explained and justified afresh to each 'new wave' of curriculum workers and teachers.

It could indeed be said that the dissemination of the ideas of the Project is well in advance of their explanation. As I observed earlier, the theories of the Project, when first published, seemed well-worn and familiar, and inextricable involvement with the career of the Schools Council cannot be the only reason. There seem to me to be two other factors. Since the inception of the Project in 1966, the members of the team, both qua members and as individuals, have published a steady stream of books, articles in educational and other publications, and contributions to the 'trade' newspapers and conferences, which revealed and explored parts of the research and its models. In 1967 James Britton edited *Talking and Writing*, which contained, besides his introduction, an article by him entitled 'The Speaker' which discusses the Participant/Spectator roles in language, one by Nancy Martin on 'Stages of Progress in Language', and another by Harold Rosen on 'The Language of Textbooks', containing his now well-known observation that this language 'looks at children across a chasm'. I have already mentioned *Language, the Learner and the School* (1969) where the word 'curriculum' creeps in for the first time and the slogan 'Language across the Curriculum' is coined. Britton's own *Language and Learning* followed in 1970, and was adopted as an Open University text. As a result of endorsing his views (and indirectly those of the Project team) the writers of E262, *Language and Learning*, (part of the Second Level Educational Studies Course of the Open University) established these views as part of the mainstream of educational discourse. Further, Britton's article 'What's the use? A schematic account of language functions', first published in the *Educational Review* in 1971, was included in the reader for this course, *Language and Education*, and thus one of the Research team's two models gained a wide currency. There followed, in 1973, Harold and Connie Rosen's *The Language of Primary School Children*, and *Understanding Children Writing* by Tony Burgess (an officer of the development project team) and others, and *Understanding Children Talking* by Nancy Martin appeared in 1975. The three last were published in a popular format by Penguin Books. These are just some of the major titles of the books; I will forbear to list all the articles!

It would not, I think, be unfair to the other team members to infer that the prime mover and sustainer of the Project and its theories has been, and is, James Britton. Even before the Project was set up officially, he had developed his 'participant/spectator' distinction (from an idea of D.W. Harding's in *Scrutiny* as long ago as 1937) in an essay in

*Studies in Education, the Arts and Current Tendencies in Education* which he edited in 1963. This distinction has remained unmodified throughout his writings, the articles from the Project team, and in the Projects models themselves, and forms the first crucial theory of the research. All the other categories of language function on which the team's analysis of writing depends proceed from his early work on this distinction, although he himself was (and I would maintain, still is) mainly interested in 'language in the spectator role' — the 'creative' and literary uses of language. It is in this initiating and controlling influence of Britton that the second factor of explanation for the widespread knowledge and dissemination of the ideas of the Project is to be found. When the Government's 'Committee of Enquiry into Reading and the Use of English' was set up in 1972, James Britton was a committee member. When its report, popularly known, of course, as the Bullock Report was published in 1975, his by now well-known 'voice' and emphasis could be detected, chiefly in Chapters Four and Twelve, but behind many more. Chapter Four was called 'Language and Learning'. the title of his book, and Chapter Twelve 'Language across the Curriculum'. Although the Bullock Report is mainly about reading, it was Chapter 12 which caught the popular imagination, possibly because it fitted current ideas about curriculum integration and 'the unity of all knowledge' — topics to which I shall return in greater detail in subsequent chapters. At any rate, it was not long before the inspectors of the Inner London Education Authority and other official bodies were demanding that the schools in their areas should draw up and implement 'Language across the Curriculum' policy documents. Conferences were called, courses instituted, briefing meetings held at which members of the Writing Research Unit, or members of the London Association for the Teaching of English (often synonymous) initiated teachers into the theories and models of the Project. The 'movement', under its banner, had taken off at last.

At first glance it seems ironic that an idea hatched out of the 'growth and personal development' model of English teaching in the 1960s should mature as a popular interdisciplinary movement in the mid-seventies, in an educational climate once again plagued by worries about 'standards' and basic skills, and as a result of the publication of a Government Report in response to those concerns. But, though it may sound unduly cynical, it is my belief that the movement is popular precisely *because* its slogan sounds like a solution to our educational difficulties. As I hinted earlier, the members of the Project team and their associates in the LATE and elsewhere have worked so long with the theories which underpin 'Language across the Curriculum' that they underrate their difficulty and overestimate the explanatory power of the slogan. Like most slogans in education and elsewhere it makes a good rally cry, but its meaning is not evident without further unpacking. This is borne out by my reading of the 'fringe' literature which is affected by the work of the Unit but not 'of' it. Here the category names of the Project's models are used without explanation, or even quotation marks to distinguish them from accepted terms in linguistic or educational discourse; — 'spectator role', 'participant language', 'transactional', 'expressive', 'sense of audience', — are trotted out glibly without reference to the models to which they belong. It comes as no surprise to find that many schools drawing up a 'Language across the Curriculum' policy have no coherent ideas of what it should contain, and indeed many to whom I have spoken think it concerns standards of spelling and punctuation or 'Good English' across the disciplines.

But a study of what the Project is really concerned with reveals on the contrary an animosity towards the latter concept, and distinct coolness about spelling and punctuation. Nor does it approve a 'skills' approach, or 'standards', at least in the sense that they worry employers and some parents. As fully-fledged Curriculum Theory its claim for language is on a different plane. This, put simply, is that 'language gives shape to all learning'. In addition, language is to be seen through a particular model, and this model has pedagogical implications for all teachers, regardless (and I use the word advisedly) of the discipline they teach.

I shall go on to describe and analyse the work of the Unit in the Chapters which follow, but because this work spans twelve years and a great deal of published work, I do not confine myself to the two official Schools Council publications, but draw freely on the whole 'corpus' in order to expand and explicate the work of the Project team. Since the Project, in dealing with the nature of language and its relation to learning, necessarily reaches out into other theoretical areas, I endeavour to tease out these connections and their implications.

But, because it is a Curriculum Project, the project has further interest than the theory it is hypothesizing, or the sub-theories it implies. Is it good (in the sense of scientific) theory? Is its model satisfactory? Was the research procedure properly carried out? Above all, is it the kind of curriculum project that is needed, and can teachers use its findings? I therefore attempt, in my final chapter, to critically evaluate the Writing Research Project as *Curriculum* reseach and development.

# Chapter One

# Design and Development of the Project

---

**The mapping of the research area and its hypotheses**

In 1965, that matrix of all the early Schools Council projects in English, 'Working Paper Number Three' had, as we have seen, pinpointed the problem areas for research. It saw the needs of research into children's writing in these terms:

> 'To do for writing what we have suggested for speech and reading: to analyse the abilities required for written communication (e.g. sentence length, vocabulary, reading or oral attainment, and the specific demands of spelling, punctuation and paragraphing.) . . . to research into the *development* of writing ability. What can pupils achieve at the ages of 6, 9, 12, 15? At what stage do different genres become possible for children (a) when left to themselves, (b) with good teaching? . . to ascertain the range and kinds of personal writing and the relation with impersonal writing; . . . to know the advantages of "experience-centred" as distinct from "language-centred" teaching of composition; . . . to know how to teach children to translate the emphasis, tone and intonation of spoken English into effective written English' (p.13)'.

These were seen as English teachers' concerns, but the Working Paper had also, remarkably, addressed some of its questions to problems of language in general in the curriculum. In accepting the above quoted aims as their starting point, the members of the Writing Research team, who were all English teachers, also shouldered the concern of the report with the problems of language across all the subjects of the curriculum. They saw the scope of their research project as interdisciplinary, and language development as the responsibility of all teachers, not merely that of the English specialist. Their inquiry would be into the development of all abilities in written language.

But clearly, research into 'written language' *tout court* would be far too amorphous, since the term, like 'language' itself, exists only as a convenient abstraction, different facets of which are illuminated by philosophy, linguistics, psychology and the social sciences. To choose to concentrate on one aspect is necessarily — logically — to exclude others. The team chose to concentrate on 'discourse'; or language as human behaviour, and set themselves the task of evolving 'a theory of discourse.' But even here distinctions had to be made. It is possible to construct many such theories, all based on different premises, depending on whether the initial interest is in discourse as social behaviour (sociolinguistics and sociology), individual mental behaviour (psycholinguistics and psychology) or historically evolved cultural behaviour (ethnomethodology and anthropology). Although the team borrowed eclectically on a wide scale from these related disciplines, their major preoccupation was intra- rather than interpersonal language. This bias was to have a major influence on all aspects of the research project.

Within this psychological model, the project members were most interested in the connection between language and thought, or, more precisely, language as 'symbol' or 'representation' — the 'interface' between the mind and reality: 'Man acts in the world of reality by means of, or in the light of, his representation, cumulatively built, of the world as he has experienced it.' (*The Development of Writing Abilities,* p.78). In taking this as the attribute which distinguishes man from beast, they follow Cassirer:

> 'Ernst Cassirer pointed out that, of all the animals man alone responds with systematic *indirectness* to the signals he receives from the world around him. All animals have systems of nerves bringing in such signals, and other systems carrying out their responses. In man however, there is as it were a *third* system shunted across those two — the symbolic system. From the incoming signals man *represents to himself,* cumulatively, what his world is like, and his responses are thereafter mediated by that world representation . . . accumulating a 'retrospect' he projects also a prospect' (*ibid.,* p.78).

This 'symbolizing' is, according to Susanne Langer, more than an attribute; it is a positive human need. The 'new key' in her book *Philosophy in a New Key* is the exploration of this notion and its importance to aesthetic philosophy. The team make use of her 'process' and 'gestalt' approach at later points in the evolution of their theory of language. But the point to be noted here, as reinforcing the chosen emphasis on the psychological model of the individual, is that 'symbolizing' is an *activity* — something the individual human being actively *does:* 'Man interposes a network of words between the world and himself, and thereby becomes the master of the world'. It is no surprise to find this quotation from Georges Gusdorf, the phenomenologist, in the discussion of 'how language works' on page 78 of *The Development of Writing Abilities.* The bias of the English teacher — particularly that of the paradigm English teacher of the 60s, interested above all in 'growth and personal development' — makes itself evident here. Significantly, the achievements of sociology are selected from the same viewpoint. When a sociologist's work is approved of, it is because it 'illuminates interactions between people' and 'looks at the way individual representations fit into the jigsaw of social reality.' (p.79). Berger and Luckmann are quoted as evidence:

'The most important vehicle of reality-maintenance is conversation. One may view the individual's everyday life in terms of the working away of a conversational apparatus that ongoingly maintains, modifies and reconstructs his subjective reality' (Berger and Luckmann, 1966, p.172).

But, though it is viewed through the 'wrong end' of the telescope, sociology — particularly the 'sociology of knowledge' gains a foothold here on the Project's theory. For the process of structuring experience is the process by which we acquire knowledge, or, in the active terms preferred by the team, 'come to know'. Therefore, on this view, knowledge cannot be a body of facts handed on by the expert to the neophyte; it is an ongoing process in which the individual has to undertake responsibility for his own knowledge:

'It is a confusion of everyday thought that we tend to regard knowledge as something that exists independently of someone who knows. "What is known" must in fact be brought to life afresh in every knower by his own efforts . . . In order to accept what is offered when we are told something, we have to have somewhere to put it . . . something approximating to finding out for ourselves needs therefore to take place if we are to be successfully told' (Bullock Report, ch.4).

Knowledge is *personal,* in Polyanyi's sense, and more that that, it is essentially *subjective* — the 'knower cannot be separated from the known' (*Writing and Learning,* p.165). The project team thus accept that knowledge is socially determined, but with the curious twist that it is so through the interweaving of individual 'consciousnesses', each of which is busy construing its reality through and in contact with others. This hypothesis about knowledge obviously implies a theory of learning. If language is the primary means by which the person represents reality to himself, then it is the primary means by which he learns, for this act of representation *is* the acquisition of knwledge. Language is not only behaviour, it is *learning* behaviour; in using it the individual constructs representations in order to act in the world. The psychologist George Kelly is influential here. His contribution is to see this learning — behaviour as a constant hypothesizing system — a predictive apparatus for generating hypotheses and testing them against actuality. This 'personal construct system' polarizes reality so that we tend to perceive in 'extremes' — good/bad, general/particular, personal/impersonal, and so on.

The 'theory of discourse' would, then, be seen from the intra-personal standpoint — the individual's use of language to learn, in the sense outlined above. But this 'use' needed further division before the theory could generate research hypotheses. Kelly's 'bi-polar' constructs, linked with the reference to 'personal and impersonal' uses of language in the 'Working Paper' probably suggested the first 'cut'. But already in 1964, James Britton had differentiated two 'roles' for language. These were retained intact and formed the basis of the Project's scheme of language function. Whereas 'personal' and 'impersonal' describe *kinds* of writing or speaking, the theory of discourse demanded a distinction in terms of a speaker's behaviour, or of the function of the writing in relation to the speaker's *intention.* D.W. Harding, as long ago as 1937, had proposed such a distinction in terms of language in the 'participant' role, which was 'language for getting things done in the world', and language in the 'spectator' role. This latter was so-called because the individual, a spectator at a street accident, for instance, when freed from the need to act, brings into play in language detached evaluative responses. This happens not only when the individual is actually an 'onlooker' at events, but in his imagination, too, when he is day-dreaming or fantasizing, and in social relationships when he is gossiping or recounting experiences. This is extended to include both 'social' and 'imaginary' spectatorship in the work of the novelist, poet, or playwright. Britton's former interest had been in the 'spectator' role, for the insight it gave into literature and literary forms of language, which he had always maintained did not receive sufficient attention in schools. The project team now developed the notion further, working it into their overall theory of discourse: 'If man constructs a representation of the world *in order to operate in it,* an alternative kind of behaviour is then open to him: he may manipulate the representation *without seeking outcomes in the actual world.'* (*Development of Writing Abilities,* p.80). This leaves him free to attend to the representation itself — to the *form* of the language used, its patterns and images.

The effects of this polarization of language function were far-reaching in the development of the project's design: the obvious one was to

completely separate these two language functions and to create the
need for a link between them. But more subtly, it affected the construction of the model, and the bias of the results, as I shall endeavour
to show later. Two different sets of 'rules' or organizing processes for
these poles were postulated, the one concerned with affective structures
of the mind, the other with cognitive. The 'participant' role, in consequence, is seen as demanding the divorce of cognitive from affective
activity, the latter being in some way more 'human', no doubt principally because of the previously noted view of knowledge as 'subjective'.
It is difficult, in view of this attitude, to see how the team *could*
discuss all language uses objectively. It is my conviction that they did
not; the normative tone creeps in most frequently when the educational application of this part of the theory is delineated, or the writing
process analysed. (See, for example, *The Development of Writing
Abilities*, p.80).

As far as the Project theory was concerned, however, this polarization gave rise to the major *developmental* hypothesis: that as the child's
mental structures develop, along lines perhaps analogous to those
suggested by Piaget, Bruner and Vygotsky, his language functions also
develop in parallel. So he progresses from the inner speech 'for oneself'
as described by Vygotsky by internalizing more and more complex
modes of use. He represents experience to himself through progressively differentiated kinds of language function which keep step with
the dynamic of his mental life. But how does he do this, and what are
these functional stages? Further hypotheses were clearly necessary
before this 'hunch' could be converted into a theory. As a first step,
the 'spectator' and 'participant' roles of language would have to be
defined, for as they stood, at opposite ends of language use, and repre-
senting clearly differentiated and mutually incompatible mature language behaviours, they obviously shed no light on how these behaviours
were acquired. What was needed was a 'halfway house' to unite the two
— a function which contained elements of both 'spectator' and 'participant' language 'in embryo', so to speak, and from which each could
be shown to develop into mature language behaviour in either role.

But how to characterize this 'matrix' from which all other functions
grow? The team seized on an idea of the anthropologist Edward Sapir:

'It is because it is learned early and piecemeal, in constant association with the colour and requirements of actual contexts, that
language, in spite of its quasi-mathematical form, is rarely a purely
referential organization. It tends to be so only in scientific discourse,
and even there it may be doubted whether the ideal of pure reference is ever attained by language. Ordinary speech is directly expressive, and the purely formal pattern of sounds, words, grammatical

forms, phrases and sentences are always to be thought of as compounded by intended or unintended symbolisms of expression, if they are to be understood fully from the standpoint of behaviour . . . There is no danger that the expressive character of language will be overlooked. It is too obvious a fact to call for much emphasis . . . that almost any word or phrase can be made to take on an infinite variety of meanings seems to indicate that in all language behaviour there are intertwined in enormously complex patterns, isolable patterns of two distinct orders. These may be roughly defined as patterns of reference and patterns of expression.' (Sapir, 1961, pp. 10-1).

'Expressive' was therefore, on this basis, the term chosen by the Project team to stand for the 'personal everyday undifferentiated language in which we exchange opinions, attitudes, beliefs and immediate preoccupations'. Thus what is said 'reveals as much about the personality and state of mind of the speaker as it does of the events spoken about. It is defined as 'language close to the speaker', and, because it is 'free to follow the contours of thought and the shifting focus of attention', it is comparatively inexplicit, – fully comprehensible only to those who know the speaker.

But more importantly for the Project's theory, the 'expressive' came to be seen as the mode in which 'we are likely to rehearse the growing-points of our formulation and analysis of experience. Thus we may suppose that all the important products and projects that have affected human society are likely to have been given their first draft in talk between the originator and someone who was sufficiently in the picture to hear and consider utterances not yet ready for a wider hearing' (Britton, in O.U. 1972). In the Project's theory of the connections between language and learning, the expressive is thus found to be of central importance, as being more characteristic of the way in which an individual thinks when he is by himself, and therefore the form in which he is likely to try out ideas and hypotheses. But it is also central to the *developmental* thesis too. It is the *sine qua non* of language development: 'the intimate context, for the child, may be necessarily the matrix of his language development. It might not be merely empirically difficult but in point of fact *logically* too, to envisage any other starting point' (*Development of Writing Abilities*, p.140). So the 'expressive' is not merely a desirable use of language in education; it is *essential*. The notion of the expressive unites the two theories of language description and language development.

Obviously though, more 'filling out' was necessary. The threefold map of function 'participant – expressive – spectator' was still too crude either as a developmental or descriptive hypothesis. Since the developmental hypothesis stated that the individual's language develops by progressive differentiation of function from a matrix, any categorization between matrix and pole would have to reflect this development as a *continuum*. Also, since the categories or functions so differentiated between 'expressive' language and 'participant' language, and between 'expressive' and 'spectator' language were held to reflect the individual's mental processes and 'follow closely the dynamics of cognitive and affective development', they could not be merely descriptive; they had — and again this is a logical point — to reflect the stages of growth. There was a further difficulty with the 'spectator' pole. Its previous full characterization, by D.W. Harding and then by James Britton, as including real, imaginary, and literary spectator-language, had already given it a developmental division. It clearly contained already more than was designated by the term 'personal'; what had come to be called 'creative' uses of language clearly had their place here too. (There was no such difficulty with the 'participant' role; both authors' literary predilections ensured that it remained uncharacterized other than as 'language for getting things done in the world' and could be taken as a synonym for 'impersonal'.) It was impossible to 'cut' the two roles so that the 'matrix' category of the expressive could be interposed between them. The terms 'spectator' and 'participant' were therefore retained as describing 'two modes of language use' but another category system would have to be constructed which was capable of bearing sharper functional distinctions, and which furthermore could be used to show how the individual's language use *developed* from the undifferentiated 'expressive' towards the two poles.

Here once again, the work of Sapir suggested the solution. The project team this time moved from his description of all speech as expressive, to his idea that the component parts of speech — of reference and expression — vary according to the demands of the communicative situation. When the need to communicate increases, speech becomes more explicit at the expense of its expressive features. The team extended this description to make it fit movement from the expressive in the opposite direction towards 'the literary spectatorship' of Harding, which they designated 'the poetic'. At the extreme of this mode, developmentally speaking, expressive features are modified so that the utterance becomes 'a verbal construct' — a work of art. The linguistic rules of use, at their least demanding in the expressive, have to be progressively internalized in order to acquire mastery of the functions on either side of it.

The Research Unit had now worked out a 'dynamic' three-term scale with which they could differentiate the language processes and distinguish one utterance from another. But there still remained some problems here. Not only was it still rather a blunt instrument, but the

categories — and the major hypotheses — had so far been worked out
in relation to the process of *speech*; the brief of the Project was to
study the *writing* process:

> 'Our task was to create a model which would enable us to character-
> ize all mature written utterances, and then go on to trace the devel-
> opmental steps that led to them' (*ibid.*, p.6).

Clearly the identification of these categories of speech with categories
of writing would have to be established. But this in itself would still
give only a correlation between *mature* written utterance and *mature*
spoken utterances, whereas the team needed both to classify the
developing writing process in schoolchildren, and in some way to relate
*kinds* of composition set as tasks in school with ways of composing.
The solution to these difficulties (though as I shall show in a later
chapter, it was at best a partial one, and in the case of the 'expressive'
very problematic) was to be found in an aspect of discourse so far
hardly considered — that of *situation*, or context. Since the project
team's preferred standpoint was, as we have seen, psycholinguistic and
intra-personal, the notion of the social determinants of function had
hardly arisen. The team had up to this point been content with Lyons'
notion of context as 'that of "the universe of discourse" in Urban's
sense. Under this head I include the conventions and presuppositions
maintained by "the mutual acknowledgement of communicating
subjects" in the particular type of linguistic behaviour' (Lyons, 1964).
Now, in trying to adapt these theories to the writing process, they
found a link through *situation*. Again the notion derived from Sapir:

> 'Clearly the degree of difference between speech and writing will
> vary a good deal, partly according to the demands of the situation
> . . . and partly according to social conventions . . . Expressive lan-
> guage interested us particularly both because it represented some
> overlap between speech and writing, and because, looked at develop-
> mentally, it seemed to be the mode in which young children chiefly
> write' (*Development of Writing Abilities*, p.11).

This seemed not only to guarantee the link between the speaking
and writing process, but generated a hypothesis based on the writing
process *per se*. The idea of the 'context' of writing, in which it is strik-
ingly different from speech, namely in its solitariness and the absence
of its addressee, caused the project team to speculate, again from an
intra-personal viewpoint, about how the writer regards the reader of his
product, and how this affects the process of production. George Mead
had suggested, in *Mind, Self and Society*, that the internalizing of an

audience was an essential part of all thinking. Man begins by 'internalizing' individuals and finally internalizes a 'generalized other' who represents society. Although this is a sociological concept, the team adapted it to apply it to the psychological notion of how the writer sees his reader, which they called the 'writer's sense of audience'. This 'sense of audience', it was conjectured, would profoundly affect the way a writer saw his task, and the means he took to produce it. It was seen in terms of a *relationship*, but one in which the viewpoint of the writer was the relevant criterion in accounting for the modification of the writing process:

> It is revealed by the manner in which the *writer* expresses a relationship with the reader in respect to his (the writer's) undertaking' *(ibid.*, p.65).

These 'ways of seeing' could thus be categorized, and evidence of a mental process taken directly from the written product. Written texts could now be assigned on the basis of two different categorizations of discourse, one of *function*, and one of the writer's *'sense of audience'*. Furthermore, since both were seen as developmental, they could be correlated, and their effects as variables in the 'writing situation' estimated.

There were obviously many more of these 'variables' in the 'context of situation', as the team realized. In their account of their preliminary discussions, they mention 'degree of involvement' in the task, 'the teacher's expectations', the 'individual's language resources'. However, the major hypotheses completed, and the general delineation of the research area plotted, it was decided that the pressing need now was for a refined model of 'function' and 'audience' on the basis of which scripts could be assigned and implications for educational practice elucidated.

## The design and data of the Project
### The model for 'function'

That speech moved outwards from the 'expressive' towards the 'communicative' or towards the 'poetic' according to the demands of the situation provided the basis for the Research Unit's first model, that of 'function'. But it was clearly necessary to subdivide these categories if they were to reflect the multiplicity of demands made upon writers and the variety of tasks they undertook. Also the notion of development from the comparatively 'rule-free' expressive to the specific and different 'rules of use' of the two poles, necessitated intermediate categories on the way. Most of the work in the analysis of discourse-function had been, as we have seen, concerned with speech, and it was again to work in psycholinguistics that the team turned for help here.

Roman Jacobson (Sebeok (ed.), 1960) had suggested that there were six discernible functions of language, emotive, conative, referential, phatic, poetic and metalingual. This list is derived from the nature of discourse seen from a linguistic point of view. Any speech situation consists, in its essentials, of an *addressor*, (the person speaking), and *addressee* (the person spoken to), a *message* passing between them, a *contact* that joins them, a *context* to which the message refers, and a *code* which governs the way the message is constructed, and how it refers to the world. Each of the functions quoted above is the result of a focus on one or other of these features of the speech situation; the *emotive* when the focus is on the *addressor*, the *conative* when it is on the *addressee*, the *referential* when the *context* is uppermost, the *phatic* when it is the *contact*, the *poetic* when emphasis is on the *message*, and the *metalingual* when it is the features of the linguistic *code* that the utterance is most concerned with. Clearly in any utterance the focus will shift from one function to another as the various components of the situation move in and out of the speaker's attention. Jacobson therefore conceived the idea of a 'hierarchy' of functions so that for any utterance, it is possible to pick out a 'dominant' function. Dell Hymes (Fishman (ed.), 1968) had accepted Jacobson's model, but thought it necessary to subdivide the 'referential' or 'focus on context' into 'referential' and 'situational'. The team found these seven types very useful in extending their basic model. ('Communicative' became 'transactional' to avoid confusion, since any use of language could be said to 'communicate' in some form.) They did not find it necessary to further define 'the expressive', since it was conceived of as a matrix, but saw it as analogous to Jacobson's 'emotive' — the focus of function on the 'addressor'. Dell Hymes had also thought the term 'expressive' better for this function, and the team thought it accorded better with the description they had taken from Sapir. Though 'the poetic' and its focus on 'the message' already existed as one pole of the model, it was impossible to take over the rest of Jacobson's functions without distortion, since the Writing Research Model had to reflect the writing process and its functions from the viewpoint of the *writer*, whereas Jacobson's were derived from the analysis of discourse *itself*. Then too, differences between written and spoken discourse made the further refinement of some functions paramount if the model was to be a sufficiently precise instrument of differentiation — 'referential', or even Dell Hymes' 'referential' and 'situational' were plainly too broad as divisions of transactional writing; 'metalingual' seemed applicable to both poetic and transactional. On the other hand, the 'phatic' function seemed to play little part in writing — certainly not enough to feature as a function in the model. The 'conative' could help to differentiate 'the transactional' but obviously if this latter was to cover all the uses of writing 'for getting things done in the world', the *kinds* of trans-action would have to be worked out more specifically.

A reading of James Moffett's *Teaching the Universe of Discourse* revealed a way of making these subdivisions through the relation of a writer to his topic. This relation, which Moffett calls the 'I-it' scale, was a developing one, which also meshed with the Project team's ideas. It was worked out as a 'scale of abstraction', the first category of which most closely resembled 'the structure of external reality', the last 'the structure of man's mind'. Moffett had four categories: record, report, classificatory, and theoretical. The team expanded these to seven, since the last two did not seem fine enough to reveal develop-ment. The 'classificatory' category was subdivided into 'generalized narrative', 'low-level analogic' and 'analogic', and the 'theoretical' into 'speculative' and 'tautologic'. It was felt that these further divisions gave a better picture of the kinds of function most prevalent in the school situation.

The subdivision of the 'poetic' was much more problematic. There were no clues to be gathered from psycholinguistics, and, since the team had taken its stand on writing as psychological process, aesthetic philosophy could be of little help, although Susanne Langer's insight helped to integrate 'the poetic' within the whole scheme of language use. A partial solution was found in the work of Jurgen Habermas (1971) and John Searle (1972), in the idea that linguistic competence embraces two sets of rules, 'rules of grammar' and 'rules of use'. The project team extended this to cover two different procedures for the 'de-contextualization of human experience'. On the transactional side, this decontextualization reflects cognitive organization, a growing awareness of 'categorial differences between subject/object, outer/inner speech, private/public world' (Habermas). One of the intersubjectively recognized rules is then, 'piecemeal contextualization'. But on the poetic side, the opposite obtains: The writer must resist such piece-meal contextualization. His 'verbal object' is a thing deliberately isolated from the rest of reality: to respond, the reader must con-textualize only *after* he has reconstructed the object in accordance with its internal complexity. 'From this conception of 'global contextualiza-tion' we derive sub-categories of poetic utterances' (*Dev. of Writing Abilities,* p.86). So the first task is to designate a piece of writing *as* poetic, as concerned with communicating a message through the total verbal construct. Then it can, if necessary, be related to a secondary *participant* function, according to what the author intended the 'global contextualization' to achieve; thus it could be poetic (conative), like Orwell's *Nineteen Eighty-Four,* poetic (informative), poetic (expressive), and so on. However, these subdivisions were not thought to add very much to the classification of school writing, and so were not included in the model designed for the briefing document. One further division remained to be made before the 'model of function' was complete. Since the model so far was designed to cover the whole range of writings in general mature use, it was thought necessary to include function categories that could represent either functions peculiar to the school situation, or childish uses of language that had no adult counterpart, and perhaps disappeared after serving their developmental purpose. These were therefore included under the headings 'immature categories' and 'special categories'.

### The model for 'sense of audience'

In attempting to categorize 'the expectation of a writer as a response to the expectations of his reader', or the writer's 'sense of audience', the project team found little in existing work of very much help to them. M. Joos, in *The Five Clocks*, distinguished five types of situation which affect the speaker's language and the hearer's response. This scale (intimate-casual-conversational-formal-frozen) did not however, discriminate finely enough between *readers* or between *writers* to be of use to the project. The team were looking for a model which would cast light on the development of the child's sense of audience from 'speech for himself' through intermediate categories to an unknown public, which achievement would reflect his maturing sense of 'the generalized other'. It would have to contain, therefore, both audience categories which embraced mature adult conceptions towards which the child was reaching out, and those specific to the child's situation as an 'apprentice' in school: in other words, categories which characterized the teacher-pupil relationship. For the part of the scale beyond the school relationships James Moffett's 'I/You' scale, which mapped the increasing distance between the addressor and his addressee was a useful parallel. But for the specifically 'school-based' categories the team decided to differentiate between the different roles of the teacher, both towards the individual pupil and the whole class, since it is for the most part the teacher who both defines the task, initiates it, and evaluates the result. Therefore it is upon the teacher-as-reader that the classification concentrates, although since what is at issue is a *relationship*, the categories are expressed in terms of both writer and reader. The former is, however, the complementary relationship.

There are five categories in the model for 'audience', of which the last — 'additional categories' — includes two subdivisions for scripts that are difficult to classify, either because they seem to have been written for no discernible audience at all, or because they have been directed to a named or 'virtually named' person other than the teacher.

The first category — *'self'* is 'writing from one's own point of view without considering the intelligibility to others of that point of view' — a written version of 'inner speech'. This class of writings has no subdivisions. The second, *'teacher'*, includes, as we would expect, the largest number of subdivisions since it is with school writing that the Project is concerned. These are: 'child to trusted adult' — where the pupil relies on the understanding of the teacher (as an extension of the parent) in a personal relationship; 'pupil to teacher general, (teacher-learner dialogue)', where the child relates to the teacher *as* a teacher and attempts to meet his idea of what the teacher expects of him in this particular task; 'pupil to teacher, particular relationship', based upon a shared interest in the context, and 'pupil to examiner' where the teacher's testing role is uppermost in the writer's mind. The third category shows the writer beginning to go beyond the confines of the teacher audience: 'wider audience, known'. It has three subdivisions. In the first, 'expert to known layman' the writer is directing his utterance to an audience which knows less about his topic than he himself does, but it is an audience which is known to him. The second, 'child or adolescent to peer group', is self-explanatory, and in the third, 'group member to working group', he is likely to be writing as part of the ongoing activity of his class. In the fourth category, 'unknown audience — writer to his readers or unknown public', the writer is attempting to go beyond the confines of school to reach the wider public outside, for a variety of reasons and with a variety of means. The categorization does not necessarily imply success — the criteria for inclusion is the writer's *intention*.

The two models just described, (a diagram of both is included at the end of this chapter) of 'function' and 'audience', were the two dimensions of 'writing as process' schematized by the Project team in order to classify children's written scripts and draw conclusions therefrom for curriculum practice. But before describing these conclusions and in order to understand their scope, we must first look more closely at the data on which the Research Unit worked.

### The data

The kind of material collected was obviously crucial for the testing of the central theory and its hypotheses, since the data was to be written scripts from children in secondary schools, each one in its way a small *fait accompli*, and observations in support of the theory could only be made by examination of completed writings. Children were not to be interviewed for the research stage of the Project, nor observed actually in the process of writing. Therefore, as the purpose of the project was to relate the 'audience' and 'function' models to pupils' progress in the secondary school and to their work in the various subjects of the curriculum, it was important to preserve a 'by subject' classification of the data both to represent school written work as widely as possible across the disciplines, and for comparison with the 'subject-free' classifications. It was also essential to collect data across the whole secondary school age-range in order to plot progress, and furthermore to sharpen the age-distinctions by gathering it from the first, third, fifth and seventh years. In addition, the whole ability range had to be represented, as well as all types of schools.

Accordingly, 2122 scripts were selected from 500 boys and girls from eighty-five classes in sixty-five schools. These were sixteen secondary school (513 scripts), fifteen comprehensive schools (331 scripts), twenty grammar schools (722 scripts), five direct-grant schools (257 scripts), seven independent schools (254 scripts) and two colleges of further education (45 scripts). Although scripts were submitted from over twenty curriculum subjects, in many of them the numbers were so low that they had to be grouped, which meant that little of value would emerge about them. Only English, history, geography, science and religious education could be examined independently. Teachers were asked to include with each set of class work details of the task set, and comments on the classes' ability in their subject. Each script had these details reproduced with it to act as a further guide to assessors. The scripts were 'scrambled' and re-assembled in sets of a hundred to be processed. Eleven teachers were invited to be 'briefed' and to assess the scripts; seven of these were selected as assessors. Working with three judges to each script (two teacher-assessors and one research-team member), the Research Unit completed the assignment of scripts by 'sense of audience' and 'function' by the autumn of 1971. The second 'developmental' stage of the Research project had proceeded alongside work on the models, and collection of data was completed also by 1971. A report on this, 'the development in writing of three hundred children in five schools' was promised, but as yet we know nothing of its findings. The 'Writing across the Curriculum' project was formed to disseminate the findings of the Research Project and examine its implications and practical applications. It therefore provides nothing new in the way of data, although its conclusions will be discussed in the next section.

## Implications for Curriculum Practice

I shall analyse the results of the Writing Research Project in a later chapter. What I shall be concerned with here are the broader implications of the project for teachers and others involved in curriculum planning, as seen by the project team. These fall into two categories: the implications for the curriculum as a whole if their theories are proven, and those which follow for classroom practice as a logical application of the theories.

In the first group, those seen as of most importance by the Writing Research Unit follow from their central hypothesis regarding the role of *expressive* talk and writing in learning. Convinced of the educational importance of such language activity, the team were very disappointed when the results of categorizing by function showed only 5.5 per cent of the sample − 109 scripts, − to be in the 'expressive' category, and much of this was in English of Religious Studies. If it is true 'that expressive writing, in carrying forward the expectations and resources of expressive talk, is likely to be both the most accessible mode for younger writers and the key to developing confidence and range in using written language', (*ibid.*, p.142), then its absence gives serious cause for concern. The team proposed two courses of action; the first, tha language policies be developed by groups of different subject teachers within a school for implementation by the whole staff (a cause taken up by the Bullock Report as 'Language across the Curriculum'), the second that local authorities and professional associations should lend their strength to these innovations by organizing conferences and courses which 'cut across the curriculum boundaries', to look at the relationship of 'writing and talking to thinking and learning'.

The implications of this particular hypothesis for curriculum organization, only lightly hinted at in such phrases as that quoted above in *The Development of Writing Abilities*, are hammered home in *Writing and Learning across the Curriculum*:

> 'Writing which is much closer to talk than most school writing is at present should be encouraged right through the child's years at school − and across the whole curriculum. We believe that such writing would free the writer to think in writing and to learn through using written language in the same way that he already uses talk' (p.61).

The functions established for the writing process are both independent of school subjects and applicable to all of them. Learning in science is facilitated by the use of 'personal, everyday language' which draws on 'first-hand experience', no less than history or English. This change in the view of what knowledge *is* − from its being seen as an objective body of facts to be handed on, to 'experience which has to be recreated in the mind of every knower' means that a learning environment has to be established which encourages the growth of this process: 'The demand for impersonal, unexpressive writing can actively inhibit learning because it isolates what is to be learned from the vital learning process − that of making links between what is already known and the new information' (p.26). This learning environment will be preferably *interdisciplinary*, and one in which children 'can make choices from the outset and settle for themselves what they want to work at.' Programmes in all subjects must 'match the children's interests and intentions or their views about what is important' (p.165). This emphasis on children programming their own learning will help to foster creativity, not only in 'traditionally more personal subjects like English' but in the sciences and history. Linked with the team's notion of 'creativity' is their view of the role of the imagination: 'We believe that the mental act of envisaging or imagining (which we do continuously in conversation about people, events and ideas) has in school work been largely restricted either to the exploration of personal fantasies in English lessons, or to the lower streams . . . as a form of mental activity which is regarded as inferior to generalizing about the facts and to ordering them logically and concisely' (p.86). But imagination is 'the mental process which enables a person to make his own connections, whether this happens to be in the sciences or in the arts . . . unless we provide many opportunities all over the curriculum for children to use their imaginations more extensively, their knowledge will remain inert' (p.87). These opportunities increase wherever the influence of English spreads to other subjects, usually by way of integrated curricula. Then it becomes clear to teachers of other subjects that all work can be brought within the orbit of imagination and creativity through the personal reconstruction and interpretation of events which *is* expressive language.

This changing notion of progress in language and learning has another implication, further reinforced by the team's findings in the 'sense of audience' categorization. If knowledge cannot be regarded as the transmission of bodies of facts from the initiated to the uninitiated, the *ways* in which children learn will be blocked by traditional 'transmission' methods of teaching. Education will have to be seen as 'a cooperative learning situation' in which the teaching/learning relationship is one of dialogue, of reciprocity. But when the project data was processed, it was found that most writing in the sample fell into the 'transactional' function, and the 'teacher as examiner' audience category. Furthermore, the proportions grew dramatically larger in the fifth year and seventh year, and 'expressive writing' and more personal audience categories shrank into insignificance. The team concluded that the pressure of examinations therefore inhibits all other language functions; whatever the subject or potentially different mode of experience, all writing in school seems to 'grow together' towards one use of the writing process. The team therefore, whilst recognizing that examinations will not disappear, nevertheless feel that examining *procedures* need to be looked at in the light of the research findings. They recommend that other methods of evaluating language-behaviour than that

of direct measurement should be investigated, and also that achievements in all forms of language-use should not be restrained by those
performances that *are* measurable becoming the paradigm use of
language in schools.

The low incidence of expressive writing, and, at the other end of the
'participant' scale, of speculative and theoretical writing, meant that
the team's major hypothesis that writing development in either direction, to transactional *or* poetic uses, would prove to be a process of
progressive differentiation, with the expressive as the startingpoint, was
neither proved nor disproved. They expected to find a great deal of
expressive writing in all subjects in the first year of secondary schools,
and a gradual increase of the other forms throughout the age-range
with a consequent diminution of the expressive, but with a mature
version of this latter persisting for adult uses. This did not happen; not,
the team conclude, because the hypothesis was wrong, but because the
aims and objectives of the *whole* curriculum somehow narrow the
range, and discourage independent thinking. This brings me to the
second set of implications, those for classroom practice.

These centre chiefly on the team's view of the role of the teacher.
I have already indicated the team's preference for a child-centred
'learning environment' with the child 'at the centre of, and initiating,
his own learning.' From this and their view of 'expressive' talk and
writing, it logically follows that the traditional role of the teacher has
nothing to offer. Teacher-directed learning imposes a structure on the
learner, when he must be left free to perceive his own structure from
first-hand experience, or the interaction of his own everyday language
with secondary experience. The teacher therefore must be 'a partner'
in learning: he *also* learns. The 'sense of audience' categories are
invoked here, to show that lack of 'expressive' writing, – and therefore,
in the project's view, of vital links with the child's linguistic resources
– stems in schools from the fact that the bulk of writing is produced
for the 'teacher as examiner'. It does not matter whether or not this is
how the *teacher* sees himself; what is vital to remember is that this
category is a *relationship*, and this is how the child has come to regard
*his* relationship with the teacher. The child sees writing as a means of
informing the teacher of facts that he *knows* the teacher already
knows. The implications here are twofold; first the relationship of
teacher and taught must be perceived by the child to be a *dialogue*,
where each has something to contribute, and the child knows that he
*himself* is interesting to the teacher, and not merely the accuracy of
what he writes, and secondly, though evaluation clearly must take
place, it must not be allowed to constrain the whole of the child's
written output, and wherever possible, must take place in a 'learning
environment' in which the relationship with the teacher is one of trust:

'The teacher-learned relationship is *not* one of authority' (*ibid.*, p.163). This is emphasized again: teachers must see themselves as 'partners (senior parters perhaps) *rather than* authorities, so the word 'teaching' becomes hyphenated, 'teaching-learning'; education becomes more of a dialogue' (p.166) (my emphasis).

Finally, for two sorts of teachers, the implications are spelled out more clearly. First, and most obviously, English teachers must not be content merely to evoke 'personal' writing, which it is felt many of them do already. They must encourage growth towards the 'poetic' as another, and educationally equally relevant, kind of ordering worth fostering in schools. What the rules of this 'ordering' are is by no means as clear as for transactional writing, but they probably have to do with the gradual articulation of feeling in form, as Susanne Langer has shown. The English teacher must therefore provide ample opportunities for the child to develop from the 'intimate sharing of experience' with 'a known and trusted listener or reader' to a construct which 'is meaningful because the writer's handling of language makes it so' (*ibid.*, p.115). The other particular kind of teacher, the science teacher, has a choice. Either he can teach 'a body of accepted knowledge', or he can teach 'the *process* by which that knowledge is acquired'. The team believe that the way science teachers 'see' their subject is bound up with the way that they use language. If they see it as a body of knowledge, then 'transactional informational writing will be the appropriate method of expression and communication.' But if it is seen as a 'process', then self-expression and exploratory talk and language become the appropriate language uses. Unfortunately, they conclude, at the moment the former view predominates. But the team believes that a 'language across the curriculum policy' in schools should effect a gradual acceptance of the importance of the role of the 'expressive' in science as well as in the humanities.

But on this topic, *Writing and Learning across the Curriculum 11-16* ends on a note of caution. Language policies are not cure-alls; they 'should be approached with caution', because by themselves they cannot be effective: 'attempts to formulate and put into practice a language policy in a school which does not also take into account the other interconnected changes will only be tinkering with surface features and may actually make learning through language opportunities worse rather than better' (p.169). *All* the implications of the Project — theoretical as well as practical — make up a package-deal. To accept its theory of language is to accept its theory of learning and knowledge, and the changes in practice that these theories are seen by the Project team logically to entail.

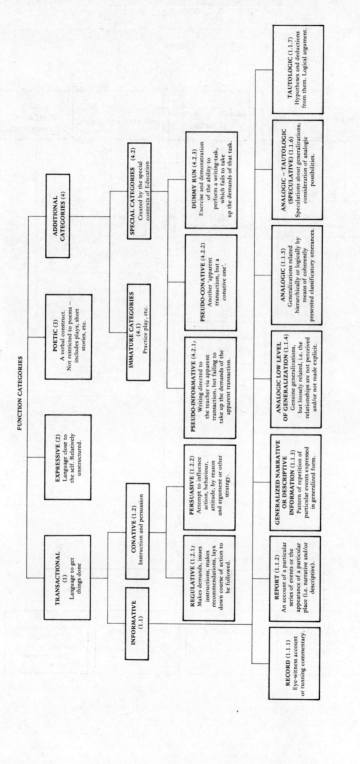

FUNCTION CATEGORIES

**TRANSACTIONAL (1)** Language to get things done

**EXPRESSIVE (2)** Language close to the self. Relatively unstructured.

**POETIC (3)** A verbal construct. Not restricted to poems – includes plays, short stories, etc.

**ADDITIONAL CATEGORIES (4)**

**INFORMATIVE (1.1)**

**CONATIVE (1.2)** Instruction and persuasion

**IMMATURE CATEGORIES (4.1)** Practice play, etc.

**SPECIAL CATEGORIES (4.2)** Created by the special contexts of Education

**RECORD (1.1.1)** Eye-witness account or running commentary.

**REPORT (1.1.2)** An account of a particular series of events or the particular appearance of a particular place (i.e. narrative and/or descriptive).

**GENERALIZED NARRATIVE OR DESCRIPTIVE INFORMATION (1.1.3)** Pattern of repetition of particular events expressed in generalized form.

**ANALOGIC LOW LEVEL OF GENERALIZATION (1.1.4)** Genuine generalizations, but loosely related, i.e. the relationships are not perceived and/or not made explicit.

**ANALOGIC (1.1.5)** Generalizations related hierarchically or logically by means of coherently presented classificatory utterances.

**ANALOGIC–TAUTOLOGIC (SPECULATIVE) (1.1.6)** Speculations about generalizations; consideration of analogic possibilities.

**TAUTOLOGIC (1.1.7)** Hypotheses and deductions from them. Logical argument.

**REGULATIVE (1.2.1)** Makes demands, issues instructions, makes recommendations, lays down course of action to be followed.

**PERSUASIVE (1.2.2)** Attempt to influence action, behaviour, attitude, by reason and argument or other strategy.

**PSEUDO-INFORMATIVE (4.2.1)** Writing directed to the teacher via apparent transaction, but failing to take up the demands of the apparent transaction.

**PSEUDO-CONATIVE (4.2.2)** Another 'apparent transaction, but a conative one'.

**DUMMY RUN (4.2.3)** Exercise and demonstration of the ability to perform a writing-task, which fails to take up the demands of that task.

## AUDIENCE CATEGORIES

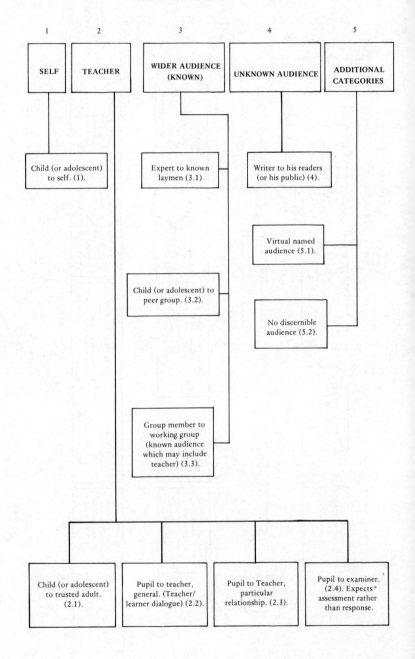

# Chapter Two

# A Critique of the Project's Theories of Language

## a) The Central Theory

Although the Project team tell us that what they are after is a 'theory of discourse', based on 'the facts of language' there are no such 'facts' of language *tout court*. The facts are different and of different logical orders, depending on what one wants to *know* about language. The 'facts' will be different for the linguist, for the linguistics expert, for the 'philosopher of language' or the 'linguistic philosopher', for the ethnomethodologist, the anthropologist, and so on.

I have already indicated that the Project team were interested in a psychological orientation for their work, preferring an intra- rather than an interpersonal approach to language function, probably because of the popularity of the new science of psycholinguistics in the 1960s when the Research Unit began its work. At this time most of the valuable studies of language-acquisition were made, and the reverberations of Chomsky's early work on transformational grammar were being felt in Europe, profoundly altering views on syntax and linguistic creativity. The previous paradigm of linguistics, that of Firth and Malinowsky which was concerned with the semantic aspect of language, or meaning, and consequently was interpersonal in its orientation, fell into temporary neglect. But the balance has been restored in the 1970s, with the growth of the new study of 'sociolinguistics', though linguists do not always accept the distinction. (M.A.K. Halliday says he had always believed that what he worked in was *linguistics*, but now people tell him that what he does is *socio*-linguistics!)

The orientation changed almost while the Project's data was being processed, and the *Writing across the Curriculum* development project shows more awareness of the social context of language. But since the development project produced no new *theories*, being mainly concerned with dissemination and reinforcement of the Research Project's findings, we need not take account of this change.

The project team tell us that they chose a psycholinguistic perspective because they were *primarily* interested in mental development:

'Since the key to our concerns — and as we saw it, to those of the classroom too — lay in an account of development, it seemed important that out categories be *psycholinguistic* in nature. They had to be related to what writers have to do, and ultimately to the part played by language and thought in the individual's mental life. Secondly, and for the same reason, it seemed important that our categories be interrelated categories . . . the overall theory of 'representation' underlying the way we have classified function, starts from this point. For our belief is that different kinds of writing, whatever may be specific to them, have their roots in the general processes of the individual's ongoing use of language' (*The Development of Writing Abilities*, p.144).

When we come to decide then, for the purpose of analysis, what kind of theory we are dealing with here, it seems that the answer should be quite straightforward. It is a *psychological* theory of language, in particular of written discourse, together with a 'systems model' of language functions as seen through the grid of the theory. As a psychological theory it is (leaving aside until the next chapter O'Connor's caveat about the social sciences) a *scientific* theory, and can be stringently assessed as such. And certainly, it has all the appearances of such a theory; it has a research programme, hypotheses are 'thrown up' and discussed, data collected and analysed, and results processed and published. A 'main developmental hypothesis' is established which is promised to be explanatory and predictive. Why, then, in mulling over the project's theories and statements, do I find that they more often than not seem to demand *philosophical* arguments and caveats?

I do not wish to assert that scientific theories should not have a basic philosophical position: it would be very difficult to construct one without at least a value-position behind it. Even theories in the natural sciences are ultimately based on a philosophical viewpoint, though it is perhaps not always articulated. But this philosophical basis does not, in good theory, enter into the actual *theorizing*; though it might influence the model, the scientist is aware of this and makes suitable statistical allowances. There is, however a fundamental difference between a *philosophical* theory and a *psychological* theory which does not appear to have been kept in mind by the research team. It is that it is pursuing different goals by radically different means. Philosophy is a *conceptual* inquiry; psychology is an *empirical* one. Therefore philosophical theory will be concerned to 'prove' itself by the conceptual analysis of *typical* cases — in this case, of language use. A *psychological* theory of language will, on the other hand, be concerned with *actual* usages, whether they are rational or irrational. The methodology and means of inquiry, and the data used, are therefore quite distinct; it is inappropriate to use the means of one on the data of the other, or to arrive at the conclusions of one by the form of inquiry of the other.

The theory of language of the Project should therefore, if it is psychological, be based on an empirical survey of what people actually *do* with language. Because the chosen standpoint is *intra-personal*, and we cannot actually inspect the contents of people's minds, their intentions, feelings, and so on, the team could only reach conclusions about these by *observing the behaviour* of the subjects, or *asking* them about their intentions, *et cetera*. Though the team admit that they regard language as a part of a person's behaviour, for the purposes of the research project categories at least, they did not *observe* the writers of the 2000 scripts that comprise the data *actually* writing, nor did they question them about their intentions. The only information they had on this score was the brief note from the teacher with each batch of *class* writings. Further, though it is allowable that *a priori* categories might be arrived at from a hypothesis about how language or discourse works, these categories should be regarded as *provisional only*, until they have been rigidly tested *empirically* and experimentally, with all that that means in terms of controls, variables, and so on. It is accounts of these sorts of procedures that we expect to find in the published account of a research project. Is that, in fact, what we do find in the *Development of Writing Abilities*?

On looking closely at this account of the design and development of the work of the project over its five years, we find no evidence of trial runs for 'fit' of the model, or of the derivation of the categories from observation. We find instead an impressionistic and subjective account of how the team evolved a 'continued mode of working' which consisted in meeting 'for a day or half a day or an evening' once a week, working on pilot scripts collected the previous summer . . . testing out any idea that seemed promising . . . focussing on the process of writing, a fuller understanding (of which) would lead to ways of construing differences between products that were psychologically meaningful' (*ibid.*, p.53). Leaving aside for the moment the question of how they derived evidence of process from product, let us look again at how the team arrived at these 'ideas' they tested out. I have shown in Chapter 1 that their method was eclectic. Though for the most part they turned to *existing* research in psycholinguistics for what they needed as the design developed, they also made use of philosophers (Langer, Gusdorf), anthropologists (Sapir), ethnomethodologists (Dell Hymes), and teachers (James Moffett). They refer to books, research papers, theses, in all these fields, but in no case, as far as I have been able to discover, did a part of the model or theory derive *directly* from empirical work by the Research team, not was it tested out under controlled conditions. What would count as empirical *evidence* for the validity of the categories was not made clear, nor indeed was any experiment which might invalidate say, 'spectator role' as a category of language, specified. So the hypotheses regarding language are not susceptible to empirical proof, and are therefore not contained within a *psychological* theory of language, and cannot be discussed and criticized within this discipline.

What *sort* of language theory, then, is it? It is *not* a *linguistics* theory, since as Britton admits, no linguistic markers have been established to pick out one language use from another:

> 'If our sets of categories prove of value to research or teaching . . . it will be essential that our original design should be completed by inquiring what linguistic features, if any, prove to be their exponents. (I am prepared, in admitting that we have not done so, to blush with shame as often as is necessary). This will involve taking scripts allotted to categories by our means – that is to say by the pooling of subjective judgments – and submitting them to linguistic analysis in search or partial correlates. Had we attempted to do this at an earlier stage, we would of course have short-circuited the experiment' (Britton in Davies (ed.), 1975).

I find it difficult to see why to develop hypotheses subjectively and then to look for linguistic correlation as confirmation *before* publishing results should be regarded as 'short-circuiting', but at any rate, it does not seem to have been done *at all*, and linguistic criteria for the categories remain unspecified. To specify would certainly have damaged the 'subjective' nature of the judgments the team seem to prefer, but would it not have made the assigning of scripts less of a hit-and-miss affair, and at the same time made them of more *practical* use for teachers? Both Roman Jacobson, from whom the team 'borrow' some categories, and M.A.K. Halliday, the originator of another function-system from a strictly sociolinguistic standpoint, do so. It is clearly easier to understand and evaluate *reasons* for judgments regarding classifications, otherwise it becomes a matter of accepting or rejecting a tenet of faith.

What we have then, in the Research Project's theory of language, is a language-descriptive theory, from the 'intra-organism' viewpoint; a theory of discourse which, when we read the justification in the *Development of Writing Abilities*, depends in large measure on persuasive argument. Is it therefore a *philosophical* argument? As I have already pointed out, philosophical discussion of language is not concerned with empirical data *about* language, or categories describing what *is* the case. It is, though, concerned with what can be said about *kinds* of statement or discourse, for example 'persuasive, emotive, descriptive, or evaluative language', but this is from the standpoint of language *itself* and not from that of the *individual's* empirical uses of language. The Project's categories are, in this respect, puzzling. As descriptive categories, they are supposed to yield *scientific* data, and indeed, this has been tabulated, correlated, and cross-referenced by a variety of scientific techniques for age, sex, subject context, and so on. But they are also, we are told, indicative of the writer's intention. Are they then guilty of the most classic of logical 'skids', the category-mistake?

Gilbert Ryle, in *The Concept of Mind,* has analysed the mistake as follows. It consists, he says, in the substitution of a *causal hypothesis* for a *functional description.* The source of the mistake is to suppose that questions about human behaviour are questions about the *causes* of the behaviour (in this case the 'intentions' of the individual), whereas they are requests for criteria, or *descriptions.* What then happens is that, in distinguishing between behaviours, one notes certain descriptive differences. These differences then become the criteria by which we distinguish one behaviour from another, in this case, one kind of language behaviour from another. But the category-mistake consists in taking these different expressions for granted, and not logically analysing them. A *cause* of the differentiation is looked for, other than that of linguistic convenience which gave rise to them, and *intention* is then postulated as this cause. Thus the categories of the Project are trying to fulfil two functions, one hypothetical and mentalistic, the other behavioural and descriptive. The confusion arises when the categories are applied to the data; the results of the scientific processing of the data, applicable only to the descriptive categories, are applied to the 'intentional' ones, and are thought to reveal statistical evidence about *processes.* Thus the philosophical/psychological standing of the project is ambiguous.

This ambiguity is further borne out by an inspection of the chapter in the research volume entitled 'The Process of Writing.' Although in many ways it is the 'key' chapter — 'process' being what the team assert they are interested in — it begins in conjecture, and proceeds by way of the insights of others (some of whom are philosophers, and some scientists), many 'we believe' and 'it seems' statements, to the exploration of hunches about the mental processes involved in writing. It is disarmingly frank:

'It is true that the inferences we can make as we read the work of children will be largely intuitive. This need not worry us. The better we know the children, the more apt our intuitions are likely to be. Often in the course of this research project, our reading of the pupils' writing led us to make intuitive judgments . . . and many of them contributed to the hypotheses and theoretical formulations that are presented in the following chapters' (p.44).

Although the team were familiar with the work of Janet Emig in America, no attempt was made to investigate by experiment what difficulties were met with during the writing process, and what stages actual composing went through. As I pointed out earlier, it is difficult to see how one could investigate the *process* of writing *empirically* without conducting experiments, but there *is* a long tradition in *philosophy* of deducing mental processes by introspection and intuition.

Proceeding to the *content*, rather than the logical standing, of the Project's theory of language, let us look more closely at its hypotheses. First, as we have seen in Chapter 1, it is based on the notion of language as *representation*; 'cumulatively built, of the world as one has experienced it, in the light of which a person "acts in the world of reality" '. This, given the individualistic framework of the theory, is unobjectionable as it stands. However, there is the suggestion, admittedly subtle here, but occurring elsewhere in the Project that the 'world of reality' is somehow different from the representation of it that we have built up through the interaction of language and experience, and further, that each individual's 'construction' of that reality is subjective and different. (This view, of course, leads directly to the view of *knowledge* as 'subjective and personal'. I shall deal with this point later as part of the Project's theory of knowledge.) That there *are* differences in the interpretation of some experiences from one person to another is no doubt true; but we can *only* recognize these individual differences because for the most part, *most* people interpret the world as we do. Unless this were so, communication would be impossible. There would be nothing in my language-representation which accorded with the experiences of anyone else.

It is also disturbing that this view gives no room to the idea of social and cultural patterns being mediated through language. The picture of the individual acting on the world through an inner organization of 'experience-through-language' is not only a lonely one, it is misleadingly partial. It takes no cognizance of the *involuntariness* of much of what we absorb from the culture and society 'ready-made' as it were, through language. There seems to be no good reason, given the eclectic nature of the study, why allowance for cultural and social influences could not have been made within the Project's framework, particularly since their omission prevents much that is relevant to the discussion of language in schools, for instance the work of Bernstein and Labov, from coming within the scope of the inquiry.

This brings me to the consideration of the team's view of the *con-*

*text* in which the speech or writing occurs. The team take Lyons' (from Urban) 'universe of discourse' and his 'context of situation' as their preferred, again *psycholinguistic*, viewpoint. But this is not very satisfactory for speech uses of the kind the team have chosen to examine, since it ignores the wider context and pressures of *society* which operate upon language, and is plainly unsuitable for writing, where 'the mutual acknowledgment of communicating subjects' in some functions has no meaning at all. But the omission is more serious since the Project is trying to analyse school writing, where the 'context of situation' (and I use the phrase here in Halliday's *sociolinguistic* sense) includes the separate disciplines or subject-matters as well as the mini-society of the classroom and the *person* of the teacher. The decision to exclude reference to 'subject' was a deliberate one; the team were looking for a way of systematizing language that would 'overarch the disciplines' and allow them to say 'whether a piece of writing in science, or a piece of writing in history, *irrespective of subject* were alike or different' (my emphasis). This was partly the result of their brief; they wanted to classify 'all mature written utterances' with a view to producing a document which would be of use to all teachers, not just English teachers. But it was also the result of their *being* all English teachers. (Or they had been; they were now university lecturers.) With a curious lack of imagination, they approached writing in all subjects as though it were writing in English, forgetting, or ignoring the fact that for the English teacher, *kinds* of writing are part of the actual subject-matter of the discipline, whereas for other teachers writing is a *means* only. Their first responsibility is to their subject-matter; language either spoken or written, is of secondary importance. (Though still important, of course, as a *means* of learning.) But the team seem to want to graft uses of language, possibly tenable in English, from their own subject-area to all the others of the curriculum, without any research into the concepts of other disciplines to find out what *kind* of language best advances the pupil's knowledge of them. Indeed, there is so little sympathy for the languages in which other disciplines report or record their concepts that they are all lumped together under the heading of 'transactional': 'language for getting things done in the world.' But what an immense variety of 'things' being done in the world is ignored by the Project team, and lurks under the 'low level transactional' percentages of the results! It is ironic that 'poetic', which describes content *and* function, and evokes most enthusiasm from the team in their description of the categories, defeats their attempts to analyse it, and the sub-categories they did devise, mostly of achieved adult genres, are left out of the assessors' brief!

Many indeed feel the dichotomy between the 'spectator' and 'participant' uses to be false, particularly linguists, who point out that *all*

language is participatory, in some sense. It does indeed seem a mislead-
ing division, particularly when the same terms are used with opposite
values by others, for instance Jerome Bruner, who talks about the
desirability of encouraging participant rather than spectator science in
schools (Bruner, 1971). James Britton's definition of 'spectator-role'
language as 'an alternative mode of action — that of operating *directly
upon the representation*, without seeking an outcome in terms of the
actual' is frankly mystifying. What other kinds of outcome can an
action have besides an *actual* outcome? If the action in mind here is
the production of an art-like construct, like a poem or a novel, is this
not 'actual'? Also, does not the construction of such an art-object
involve the writer in participating in the world of reality through his
experiences *as well as* operating on the forms of language itself? Does
not this latter indeed involve 'participation', however understood,
since though he may *choose* the form he uses to construct his poem,
the forms *from which he chooses* are transmitted by the culture
through language?

John Dixon, in *Growth through English*, reaches very similar conclusions in rather different terms. Calling the spectator/participant
role a 'crude' distinction, he gently takes James Britton to task for
concentrating his approval too exclusively on the 'spectator' role.
Many 'participant' uses, he feels, are central to English lessons: 'observing, recording, and reporting, and the complementary part, the explaining, reminding, warning, and appealing to the audience in a participant
role'. Ironically, too he feels that the emphasis on the 'spectator role'
has 'tended to narrow the definition or literature. In a more *restricted*
sense this means works of fiction which . . . in the main use the enac-
tive and narrative levels of abstraction. But in the broader and more
traditional sense, literature includes a variety of other works . . . the
imaginative writer has frequently been absorbed in more than fiction.
Some of this work, I suppose, borders on History, Politics, Ethics,
Sociology . . . I suspect that there may be an *ebb and flow* between
informative and artistic purposes . . . the careful observation of people
in action in their daily lives (Orwell); the reconstruction of key mom-
ents in their lives from statistics and documentary evidence (Defoe),
the collection and editing of a faithful record of their personal his-
tories . . . (Blythe) . .' (Dixon, 1975, p.129).

Dixon sees the 'participant' and 'spectator', or 'transactional' and
'poetic' not as alternatives of language use, but as emerging in turn in
the same piece of writing, and most linguists agree with him. Whilst
aware of this consensus, and in particular of Jacobson's 'hierarchy of
function' in which he saw a multitude of functions present in any
utterance in varying patterns of dominance, the team nevertheless
decided that it was possible to differentiate a single dominant function-

category for every piece of written discourse, even when these categories were quite closely subdivided by author's intention, and even though they recognized that intention does not remain constant throughout a piece of writing. The dangers here are first, that the principles on which the categories were differentiated became confused; Jacobson's functions were arrived at by analysing discourse *itself* for linguistic features; the team's were from the writer's viewpoint of what the writing is *for*; and second, that the categories themselves are fragmented to try to include every function, so that judgment can only be 'a subjective description of styles' as Gatherer calls them (Davies, ed., 1975). The question becomes then, why should teachers use someone else's 'subjective description of styles' rather than their own, and why should they take the project seriously if they are being asked to accept a 'grid' for language, the rationale and principles for which are unclear?

The onus was clearly on the team to show *why* they chose these categories and subdivisions rather than others; whether they were *comprehensive*, and did not distort discourse by undue emphasis on some categories rather than others; whether they were mutually exclusive; (the adult categories of the 'poetic' are poetic/conative, poetic/informative, and yet the 'poetic' and 'informative and conative' categories are at opposite poles on what is supposed to be a continuum from the central expressive) and whether they were on the same logical level. This, as I have shown, they do not appear to be.

The most problematic of all the categories is 'the expressive', which is part not only of the theory of language but also of the Project's developmental theory. 'It is' says James Britton, 'the central term in the model', and 'is taken from Sapir, who pointed out that all ordinary speech is mainly expressive, only to a limited degree referential' (Britton in Davies (ed.), 1975). But this is to distort what Sapir actually said. He was, as an anthropologist, not concerned with 'discourse' but 'language' in a global sense. What he said was that 'language, in spite of its quasi-mathematical form, is rarely a *purely* referential organization' (my emphasis). 'Ordinary *speech* is directly expressive' (again my emphasis). There would seem to be no support here for making a separate category of 'expressive language' which is different from both 'the referential' and 'the poetic', particularly since he goes on to say that patterns of reference and patterns of expression are 'intertwined in enormously complex patterns in all language behaviour.' Sapir has only two categories, preferring to keep the term 'expressive' for one of them, and not for some undifferentiated middle-ground. So too does John Dixon:

'There's an ebb and flow between poles, communication and self-expression; there's room for a more differentiated role to emerge for a time, but the *overall* organization is neither on spectator nor on participant lines; I would prefer to keep the word "expressive" . . . to indicate a pole towards which the speaker/writer may tend, or, to shift the metaphor, a weighting he may give to one of the two potentials that run through language' (Dixon, 1975, p.129).

Expressive talk is very difficult to recognize, therefore, since there is no agreement about what it *is*. The team's descriptions of it tend to be metaphysical; 'language close to the self', 'language that follows the contours of thought', 'the language of gossip and every day talk'. But 'talk' as Halliday and others have pointed out, is a complex amalgam of functions, and depends for its characterization on what the situation variables are. The team however, regard the expressive mode as the 'most natural, perhaps the most primitive of functions,' in that it uses linguistic resources 'most directly'. Leaving aside that difficult word 'natural', it is very difficult to decide what this means. If it means that the function develops first, is there any evidence for this in language-acquisition studies? Bruner and Piaget both point to 'transactional' functions of language, if we mean by this cognitively organized 'language for getting things done', appearing very early in the language-development of the child. (See, for example, Bruner, 1975).

And then, what of writing? Is 'expressive writing' *really* like expressive talk, 'resembling egocentric or social speech'? (The point is of some importance, since it is in the expressive that the team see the link between speech and writing that enables them to transfer the categories developed by linguists for speech to the writing they wish to examine.) Since the skill of writing is learned so much later than speech, and when speech is already well developed, and since there is not the 'involuntariness' about learning to write that there is in learning to speak, (indeed the verb 'learn' has a different meaning in each case) is not the comparison likely to be a forced one? And is there not likely to be little residual 'expressive' by the secondary school stage, which is the stage the Project is studying? Writing functions, after the skill has been mastered in the junior school, are usually learned in connection with a *particular context of use*. One would not therefore expect to find undifferentiated expressive writing except perhaps in personal notes, diary-writing (though many of these are written very formally) and personal correspondence. The team did not, I think, include samples of the latter in their data. Since too, there is nothing logically compelling about the categories — either we accept the team's intuitions or we do not — we can observe that mature uses of writing in our society are mainly in the transactional category, apart from the personal uses just noted. Some of this transactional writing is as formally or metalinguistically skilled as poetic writing: for example, legal documents. Both seem to be equally valuable human achievements.

## b) The language development theory

That the 'expressive' exists, and can be differentiated from the other two poles is crucial not only to the language description theory, but also to the *language development* theory. The 'expressive' is seen as the matrix from which all other  language uses develop. Failure to develop and use the 'expressive' results in subsequent failure to procede along the continuum to 'participant' and 'transactional' functions on the one hand, or to 'spectator' or 'poetic' functions on the other. Further, the child procedes by a process of *differentiation*, so it is important that all functions are presented as models for his development. Hence the importance of a variety of written tasks across all the subjects of the curriculum; each subject teacher will *distort* development if he fails to allow the child free use of the expressive, since it is by means of this kind of language that he 'explores reality' and makes his first tentative hypotheses and formulations regarding 'how things are'. But, more importantly for the language development thesis, its model is seen to be *the same* as that of the language-descriptive theory. In other words, the description of what language *is* is identical with the psychological description of how language *develops* in the child. Whereas the former could be argued for on *logical* and conceptual (i.e. philosophical) grounds, (though I believe that I have demonstrated that it is not) the latter *must* be established on *empirical* grounds, i.e. on evidence from the scripts, looked at chronologically. But was such evidence forthcoming? The team were disappointed to find that, after all their careful differentiation of categories, most of the scripts fell into the transactional function (63 per cent) and within that, the analogic level of the 'informative' sub-category. The evidence for other categories was reported as 'slight'. The team conclude:

> 'Our overall hypothesis of development as a process of differentiation is perhaps neither established nor falsified by the particular dominant pattern of the sample.'

But the developmental hypothesis could never be *proved*; scientific theories (as I discuss in the next chapter) always await the arrival of 'one black swan' and confirmation by data gives only a reasonable assumption of truth. On the other hand, failure to establish a theory by evidence, or to find *no* favourable evidence, means *certain* falsification. But the team do not abandon their developmental hypothesis, nor seek for an alternative one. Misled perhaps by the neatness and economy of their logical/psychological categories, they continue to use them in the Development project, and indeed, to behave as though some measure of proof *has* been found. The Project's scientific (i.e. psycholinguistic) theory of language development therefore lacks rigour and objectivity. The guiding ideal of disinterested experiment seems to be completely lacking. The overall impression one has is of personal charisma and intuition masquerading as scientific inquiry.

Another hypothesis, however, could have been formulated from the results of the data processing for age and function, which *could* have been tested empirically, though it would have destroyed the neat logical/psychological correlation, and necessitated the construction of another model for development *only*. This is the hypothesis that *all* the functions or styles are present and can operate at once in all age groups, but are perhaps present in a simple form at first, developing into more complex organizations as the child's intelligence, powers of conceptualization, and so on also develop. These are a *parallel series* of developments, not a 'continuum', and are clearly what Bruner has in mind in his model of the 'spiral' development of language (Bruner, 1975).

c) The theory of knowledge

I have already pointed out the avoidance by the team of any discussion of the *disciplines* in relation to language, and their belief that language use in school can be described independently of the subject context. The avoidance is deliberate: on page 9 of the Research volume they say:

'We needed therefore to find related sets of categories which would allow us to classify within a theoretical framework all the kinds of written utterance which occur in schools. In attempting this we were going beyond the views of Hirst and others who ascribe the different kinds of writing to the concepts obtaining within the various "disciplines" such as science, history, philosophy, and so on. The weakness of this view of language differences is that since they are held to derive from the different disciplines they cannot account for writings which do not fall within certain subject boundaries, and they raise endless problems concerned with what is and is not a discipline. We were seeking a system of categories which would overarch the disciplines and which would be refined enough for us to be able to say, for instance, that a piece of writing in geography and a piece of writing in science, irrespective of subject, were alike (or different) with regard to function or audience or context.'

I have shown too that such a view of language derives directly from the psychological intra-personal standpoint of the Project team (and particularly from their view of the role of the 'expressive' in thinking and learning), and that it had important consequences for the research design and the model for function, and also upon the way the team interpreted the results.

It is clear that once again this is a *philosophical* position on knowledge that the Project team are taking up, not a psychological one which can be supported by evidence. To see two things as alike is to concentrate on some features of the object concerned and ignore others; we do this all the time as we conceptualize from our experiences, seeking an organizing principle in what we perceive, collecting examples, and deducing rules and principles of order. This is part of mental activity, and we cannot will it otherwise; this activity is indeed part of what we mean by 'mind'. So in seeing two pieces of writing as 'alike' the team are *necessarily* picking out some features (say, for instance, that they both appear to be informative and addressed to the same 'audience'), and leaving out others which might *not* contribute to their similarity, namely the subject-matter, or the medium in which they were produced. They are not asserting that they are alike in every respect; this would mean that the two pieces were *identical*.

This choice of aspect is an unforced decision, but the choice of what to include and what to discount reveals the team's basic philosophical, indeed, epistemological position. This is that the process of writing, or discourse, depends on the exercise of certain mental powers, which do not relate to any particular mode of thinking, indeed are developed in the individual's private mental equipment without any reference to the public standards contained in recognized 'modes of inquiry'. Indeed, these very 'standards' and modes of inquiry are rejected as too problematical.

It is true that there is a great deal of dispute amongst philosophers regarding 'forms of knowledge', 'modes of experience', or 'realms of meaning', but no one actually disputes that there *are* publicly acknowledged fields of inquiry with their own 'languages', where terms are used differently, or are part of a hierarchy of concepts, and have rules of use which are different from elsewhere. The number of these is not static, indeed, it is changing all the time as the needs of society develop, new connections between existing fields are made and a new discipline is 'spun off'. (I referred to the way that this has happened several times this century with regard to linguistics.) The problem of deciding which forms of inquiry should be taught in schools is a constant one: we clearly cannot teach all of them. But neither can we decide to abandon them, or integrate them, or let a child's 'interest' become the guiding principle, without realizing what exactly we are doing.

We do not learn language — 'words for objects' — 'meaning-free.' In other words, language is not a label we learn to stick onto various features of the world. It comes to us, as I have already indicated, with 'meanings' built in from its public uses socially ratified. When we acquire the meaning of a term, we acquire its use; the two are inseparable, and we learn 'how to do things with words', in other words, language functions, by using words and gradually finding out what they can do. This is what I mean by saying that all language use is 'participant'; our understanding grows by using words in contexts. When we know how to use a word, we can employ it correctly; we *have* the concept. The use and the concept cannot be separated. Therefore it follows that because concepts are *public* and are ordered in various publicly-ratified ways, to learn to use language correctly *is* to enter into these public forms of understanding. It is for the *teacher* to decide the structure and sequence in which meanings and concepts are learned; the *child* does not need to know the structure of the discipline, or learn 'the rules of use' except in the sense I have outlined above. But since *logically* he cannot know the structure before he learns how to use the language of the particular inquiry or discipline, any theory which demands that 'structure is not imposed on a child' and the child must 'be responsible for' and plan his own learning, is not only not assisting his understanding, it is based on a false epistemological position. It might be objected that this is to take the team's position out of context and too far; that what they are asserting is that there are many connections between children's writings that are independent of subjects *at the school level*, and that in concentrating on the language of subjects too early we are depriving children of the opportunities to learn provided by their 'own' language, which is seen as the ordinary, everyday language of common sense: 'There is always of course, an alternative hypothesis to ours; that if you limp about long enough in somebody else's language, you will learn to walk in it' (Britton in Davies (ed.), 1975). We have then to ask the further question, what is meant by 'ordinary commonsense language'?

It is true that there are 'connections' in ordinary everyday language which do not depend on the theoretical disciplines and have no connection with them. These are the 'background' concepts of our everyday life, which we learn gradually as our commonsense perceptions of the world build up. These concepts are essential to our social and personal development; it is in the growth of these organized conceptual frameworks that Piaget and Bruner are interested, and they have mapped their organization. But these concepts are not *'learned'* in the educational sense of the word; only in the psychological sense. Normal children do not need to be taught to perceive physical objects, or that they themselves have a separate identity, for instance. The language in which we talk about these commonsense concepts is diffuse and imprecise, because the concepts are held in common and do not need to be specified clearly. They form the framework of our thinking, the basis of our daily decisions, and are seldom called in question.

But by 'ordinary commonsense language' we *could* mean the language in which we express our unthinking prejudices, our uncritical opinions about the world and our fellows; — it is not *necessarily* an evaluative term. It is the business of education to sort out the prejudices, to discipline the undisciplined modes of thinking, and to lead the child to critical, rational thinking. Education draws on the first sense of 'commonsense language' that I outlined; it builds on commonsense concepts and differentiates them into the structured, organized languages of publicly established modes of thought. It does not, however replace them; commonsense language is still needed to cope with everyday life — we all know dons who are theoretically brilliant but lacking in the commonsense necessary to organize their personal lives. Commonsense language grows and develops alongside the theoretical languages, and the theoretical returns to the common sense for its orientation.

All this, however, is not to say that theoretical languages just 'grow out of' ordinary language. Without teaching a person could avoid all such language in his life. Nor would an explanation of the concepts of theoretical language in ordinary language be of any avail, nor the exploration by the child in his 'ordinary language' of these concepts. How would he get a purchase on the theoretical disciplines unless their concepts were made available to him in some *structured* form? It is here, I think, that the team's theory of language is most profoundly wrong. In advocating more use of the 'expressive' throughout the curriculum, it is in a sense imprisoning the child in a web of commonsense concepts, for it will not be long before he must understand theoretical concepts which *cannot* be translated into ordinary language: 'to have the concept of something is to know how to employ that concept in discourse'. By the beginning of the secondary school, this differentiation is already happening: many children, for instance, do science in *junior* schools. What children will fail to develop in this concentration on the expressive to the detriment of the so-called transactional will be what Jerome Bruner calls 'analytic competence'. This does not develop, he says, of its own accord, and even if encouraged by education, will not develop in a society which does not value it. I will allow him the last word:

> 'Much of the learning of formal subject-matters in the school-setting — be the subjects "natural" as in physics or "social" as in history — depends upon the child grasping the frame of reference from which the material is being viewed . . . Insofar as these organising concepts are not clear in the communication about the events,

there is no possibility of knowing how to use the context for interpreting particular items of knowledge . . . Teaching subject matters is bound to specialize in the *metalinguistic* function as it proceeds, — directing the attention to the code upon which communication is based — involving a turning-around on what one knows in order to know it more clearly and unambiguously. I would argue that it is by this process that we learn how to represent the world in a fashion that is less dependent on context, how to think about the world in a fashion that has long recourse to a symbolic system, with occasional reference to the world of extralinguistic events, in order to check whether thought is doing right by the world. In order to be supported in this type of activity there is needed a sub-community of people who are amenable to communication in this metalinguistic mode . . . Let us recognize that this is a function of schooling, and let it be given a decent chance to work' (Bruner, 1975, pp.26-7).

# Chapter Three

# The Role of Theory in Curriculum Research:
## An Evaluation of the Writing Research Project

So far I have been talking rather loosely about 'the theories of the Project', and attempting to demonstrate whether the main theories of language and language development contained in the project are 'scientific' theories or philosophical, metaphysical ones, or a mixture of the two. But these theories are contained within a Curriculum Research project, and this raises the further questions of the role of theory, any kind of theory, in educational research, and its relation to practice.

First, can we really talk about an *'educational* theory' at all? O'Connor is sceptical. The paradigm sense of the word 'theory' he says, is found in natural science, particularly in the 'more developed' sciences like physics, or astronomy. It is more often used to refer either to *an* hypothesis which has been verified by observation, or, more usually, to a logically interconnected set of such hypotheses. If the hypothesis is correct, it will always have observable consequences; if false, the anticipated consequences will not be observed. (I used this formula myself to question the Project's developmental hypothesis.) Further, actual observation of the consequences does not conclusively establish the truth of the hypothesis, it merely renders it more or less probable:

> 'The argument: "If hypothesis H is true, then a certain fact F will be observed; and F is observed: therefore H is true"', is formally invalid. On the other hand, if the observed facts do *not* confirm the prediction implicit in the hypothesis, then the hypothesis is conclusively refuted' (O'Connor, 1957, pp.72-8).

This pattern of reasoning is the 'hypothetic-deductive' method which distinguishes most modern scientific theorizing. Its best-known advocates are probably P.B. Medawar and of course, Karl Popper. It is to the latter that we owe the distinction that O'Connor makes regarding the falsifiability of hypotheses I quoted above; he drew attention to the fact that the concepts of *verification* and *falsification* are logically asymmetric. This means that scientific laws and theories are *testable*, in spite of being unprovable, by systematic attempts to refute them (Popper, 1972). 'Falsifiability' provides a criterion for Popper and his adherents to distinguish between theories that are *scientific* and those that are not. For this reason, he rejects the claims of Marxism to be a scientific theory of the development of human society, and of psychoanalysis to be a scientific theory of human personality, since neither yields predictions that are *testable*. They are therefore, says Popper, 'non-science'. Though he is at pains to point out that this does not mean that they are non-sense (Popper, 1966).

O'Connor further points out that there seems to be general agreement amongst philosophers who write about scientific method that *scientific* theories, in the sense he has outlined, fulfil three functions: (1) description, (2) prediction, and (3) explanation. But he knows of *no* educational theory at this stage which conforms either to Popper's criterion or which fulfils these functions. If such theories are to be found, he presumes it will be in the realm of the social sciences, in psychology, or sociology. But whereas it is true that we now have a considerable body of knowledge in these areas, of 'established hypotheses that have been confirmed to a reliable degree, (which) enable us to predict the outcome of their application, and to explain the processes that we are trying to control' and which makes them theories in the 'standard scientific sense of the word', nevertheless they do not approach the physical sciences in 'their explanatory power'. They have not yet been sufficiently condensed into a 'general theory' and are not yet closely-enough tied to their supporting facts. The word 'theory' is justified for 'well-established findings in psychology and sociology' only; elsewhere in education it is merely a courtesy title (*op. cit.*, p.110). He does not, however, doubt the *need* for theory in education:

'The development of a scientific psychology has put us in the position where we no longer have to rely on practice to suggest theory. It may, of course, still do so, but it is experiment rather than practice which now suggests theory. The relationship between theory and practice has become a reciprocal one. Theory directs practice and practice corrects theory' (*ibid.*, p.109).

That we have not yet attained anything equivalent to the paradigm of scientific inquiry, though, he says, is no reason to stop looking.

Hirst (in Langford and O'Connor, eds., 1973) takes a different view of the paradigm theory for education. He agrees that the theory must be testable and explanatory, but maintains that these are necessary but not sufficient conditions. Educational theory must in addition be ethical; it must tell us what we *ought* to do. Science does not have the monopoly of reasoning; there is also *ethical* reasoning. To the obvious objection that the facts of practice cannot be derived from the 'value' of theory, Hirst replies that he can see 'no reason at this point in time against the possibility of such a logic of the mapping of the fact-value relationship,' and that he is 'encouraged by philosophical work in both mental and moral concepts' to hope for 'a set or system of rules or collection of precepts which guide or control actions of various kinds.'

My objection to Hirst's view would be that it is extremely problematic to know how (not to say contentious to assert that) an ethical theory could be testable, in anything like the scientific sense used by O'Connor and Popper. Again it could be persuasive in its reasoning, but in what sense could it be 'explanatory'? What would count as its 'criterion of falsifiability' which *could* be agreed objectively?

O'Connor and Hirst disagree only about the ethical content of an educational theory. They are agreed as to the characteristics which determine what an educational theory ought to be like. On this count, neither's paradigm fits the Writing Research project's theories exactly. We have seen in the previous chapter that there is a self-confessed psychological theory of language and learning within the Project, which can be assessed on O'Connor's criteria, and I have attempted to do so in the previous chapter. There is also an epistemological theory, which as a philosophical theory calls for argument on conceptual grounds. But these theories are contained within an educational theory that clearly depends on a value-position, namely, that written discourse of particular kinds is a valuable activity in schools, has certain desirable effects in educational terms, and if pursued in all areas of the curriculum, will have certain beneficial outcomes for both teacher and taught. That all of this is evaluative language is obvious. It is in the sense in which Hirst is using the term, an *ethical* theory. It is also prescribing what educators *ought* to do, in other words, depriving practical outcomes from the value of the theory — a classic 'is' from an 'ought'. Is this theory then an ethical theory in the Hirst sense?

The answer clearly lies in whether or not the theory is testable or 'explanatory' in the tight scientific sense, but since it is not clear that any ethical theory *can* be so tested or 'explain' any but the most general features and predict any but the most subjectively-judged outcomes, it is impossible to assess this particular theory, and even if the attempt were made, since no logical 'mapping of the fact-value relationship' is attempted by the Project team, it would be bound to founder.

Perhaps both of these philosophers are setting the criteria for an educational theory too high. Indeed, Lakatos appears to think that they set them too high for science itself:

'Popper's criterion ignores the remarkable tenacity of scientific theories. Scientists do not abandon a theory merely because facts contradict it. They normally invent some rescue hypothesis to explain what they call a mere anomaly, or if they cannot explain the anomaly they ignore it and direct their attentions to other problems . . . What then is the hallmark of scientific experiment? Do we have to capitulate and agree that a scientific revolution is just an irrational change in commitment? . . . Tom Kuhn arrived at this conclusion after discovering the naivety of Popper's falsificationism. But if Kuhn is right, then there is no explicit demarcation between science and pseudoscience, no distinction between scientific progress and intellectual decay' (Lakatos, 1970).

Lakatos' solution is to take as his paradigm not the hypothesis or theory, but 'a research programme'. This consists of a 'hard core' of laws or hypotheses, protected by a 'belt' of auxiliary hypotheses. More importantly, the research programme has a 'heuristic' or problem-solving machinery. All such programmes have within them a number of unsolved problems and 'undigested anomalies', but this does not prevent their functioning. What, then, distinguishes a scientific or progressive research programme from a pseudoscientific or degenerating one? Lakatos maintains that it is the ability to predict *novel facts* on the basis of the theory. Prediction, rather than falsifiability becomes the distinguishing hallmark of progress in research. 'When theory lags behind the facts, we are dealing with miserable degenerating research programmes.' But a judgment of what is degenerate is 'an *ethical* one, and a political one too, as the history of science shows.' Criticism also achieves a new importance; it is not 'a Popperian quick kill, by refutation. It is always constructive; there is no refutation without a better theory' (*ibid.*).

This description seems to fit educational research rather better, and even accounts for shifts of emphasis — as one programme degenerates because it 'lags behind the facts' another attracts support because it is seen to be successful at predicting what will happen. Ethics and politics also have some purchase and influence here; this accords with our idea of what *really* happens in educational research, when existing programmes appear to be suppressed or just die, and research workers jump on the bandwaggon of a new and progressive programme. Also flourishing programmes appear to be able to take any amount of 'refutation' in their stride; they digest anomalies with their 'problem-solving heuristic', usually by the formulation of an auxiliary hypothesis, which, together with the original theory, accounts for the evidence. This would all certainly seem to be true, for instance, of Bernstein's research programme through the 1960s and early seventies. Only now perhaps is it degenerating, which may be because it has ceased to predict 'novel facts' as it once did.

Does this paradigm of Lakatos match the Writing Research Project, and thus provide a basis for evaluating it as curriculum research? It does seem to be better described as a research programme than as a theory, scientific or ethical, since it contains central hypotheses, auxiliary hypotheses which protect the central ones, and has developed a powerful heuristic which, to quote Lakatos again, 'even digests anomalies and turns them into evidence'. Although linguists, sociologists and others have attacked the theories, and indeed, refuted many quite positively, the bandwaggon rolls on, aided by political backing (the Bullock Report and ILEA) and its ethical overtones; 'language is obviously central, and properly understood, may solve many of our educational problems'. Indeed, the message often seems to read that if we can only unlock its mysteries language *is* the answer to *all* our problems — 'a language for life', 'the speech of the home has a lifetime purpose to fulfil' (James Britton).

The project also has its models, constructed to show categories of language by function and audience which are designed to be a useful predictive instrument for teachers. Here too the stringent divisions that O'Connor makes between the natural and the social sciences do not apply; Lakatos cites both Newtonian physics and Marxism as instances of research programmes. The only criterion is that the theories and models which derive from them should be capable of predicting novel outcomes. Marxism failed because the facts it predicted were false. Although it predicted for instance, that there would be no revolutions in socialist countries, but only in industrially developed countries, the first socialist revolution took place in industrially impoverished Russia.

Unfortunately, one of the irritating aspects of any research programme is that it is difficult to know how successful it is going to be at generating 'novel facts' until a great deal of time and money has been spent. But it is now ten years since the Project team began work, and five since the research stage was completed, and I have not been able to find any prediction it made on the basis of its hypotheses and models which have turned out to be accurate by any objective standard. Perhaps this is unfair and the hypotheses must be given time to 'catch on'. After all, until the Bullock report gave an impetus to 'writing and learning' across the curriculum, the work of the research project team was virtually unknown outside a few 'involved' centres, and even now, the 'scientific' programme, as opposed to the popularization programme, 'Writing across the Curriculum', is encapsulated in a very expensive 'Schools' Council Research Studies' format. Then too, the promised data from the development programme, which ran for four years until 1971 in parallel with the research, and which it was hoped would confirm the developmental predictions, has not materialized, and the Schools' Council do not seem to have it in the pipeline as yet.

It is perhaps, then, premature to evaluate the Project on its 'prediction of noval facts', since we do not yet know whether one of its two main hypotheses is supported by data or not. But we can perhaps look at its methodology. I have already mentioned that the language of the Report is diffuse and impressionistic, and the picture it gives of the conduct of the research is similar. We do not get an impression of rigour in the setting up of the design; many of its features appear to have been arrived at arbitrarily. When the time came for assessors of the data to be appointed, we are told that 'eleven teachers' came to a day's briefing meeting, and seven were selected. On what criteria the selection was made we are not told, not what the subject specialisms of the chosen seven were. Were they chosen to offset the 'English' bias of the Project team? It makes a considerable difference to the credibility of the judgments arrived at to know whether this was or was not so, particularly as it was decided to use a team of three assessors per script, one of whom was to be a project team member. Further, when we look at the results, the picture is even more alarming, in view of what is *claimed* to have been established by them.

Of the total of 2122 scripts, a staggering total of 1078 were *not* given the same audience category by all three assessors, and 1428 were not given the same function-category; in other words, for audience less than a *half* were agreed on, and for function less than a third. 'So far, so good', says the Report, 'But of course we could not afford to leave it at that. We made an arbitrary decision to accept as verdicts any set of judgments that showed the equivalent of two-thirds'. Remembering that one of the judges was a project team member in each case, and could scarcely be expected to have an objective approach to the categories, this is alarming. But it was not the end of the story. There still remained 126 scripts for audience, and 384 — more than one sixth! — for function. 'For these we had a fresh assessment made by three members of the team and reduced the "no-verdicts" to 18 for audience and 130 for function' (p.107). It is difficult to see how the team can hope that the categories could be used by teachers with any success, when members of the project team and their briefed assessors found so much difficulty in assigning scripts. And yet they confidently assert 'as ways of describing written tasks, the categories yield information which promises to be useful in our attempts to understand and evaluate what goes on in secondary schools' (*ibid.*).

When we came to consider the 'across the Curriculum' brief of the team, we find that the claim to have 'examined writing in all subjects' that we find in 'Writing and Learning across the Curriculum', is a gross exaggeration. The Research report is more honest: 'Because of the limited number of scripts in many subjects we have been able to

examine only English, history, geography, science and religious education independently; all the other subjects have had to be grouped, so
there remains nothing very useful we can say about them.' So only
*five* subjects were looked at closely, and of these, English contributed by
far the largest number of scripts, 822. Science subjects, taken together,
contributed 327 scripts — 182 in biology, 84 in chemistry, and 61 in
physics. So it is on the basis of just over three hundred scripts that the
team makes its assertions about the prevalence of low level transactional writing in science in our schools!

The numbers of scripts seem to suggest something eccentric in the
collection of the data. And here we detect a note of helplessness in the
report:

'Our collectors were volunteers — that is to say they selected themselves, no doubt for a variety of reasons of which we have taken no
account. The writings were produced under a variety of circum-
stances, related to a variety of teaching objectives and methods
which again, we have no means of accounting for' (p.107).

Why *not*? — one is tempted to ask. Surely in six years it was possible
to design and execute the project, which after all is on a small enough
scale, on scientific experimental lines, taking account of all biases and
variables possible, and above all, making sure that the sample was
representative, particularly with regard to *subjects*, since so much
hinged on what would be discovered in the writing of disciplines other
than English. Then too, if the 'variety of teaching objectives and
methods' were not, on the team's admission, taken into account, how
can the writers of 'Writing and Learning across the Curriculum' assert
with such confidence that the findings of the Research Project logically imply the need for a change in pedagogy?

Since the model for function, in particular, (though initially both
models) gave so much trouble to the script assessors, one might expect
that the team would check that the model itself was not at fault;
perhaps the categories were not sufficiently clearly differentiated from
each other, or perhaps some were overfragmented. 'Poetic' is presum-
ably easy, but what of the eleven subdivisions of the 'transactional'?
In any event, it was of great importance to get it working efficiently,
since mistakes would badly distort the results. But no change in the
model was made; the main aim was to 'get a verdict' for each script,
not to get it *right*. When the results were out, the under-use of so
many of the categories was not related to possible faults in the models'
emphasis or underlying assumptions; it was explained away as the result
of 'curriculum and examination pressures' in the schools, which, and
the teachers in which, we have just seen that they 'had no means of

accounting for'. Warning bells for the scientific method — *any* scientific method — ring louder. *Any* scientific basis for the Research programme proves, on investigation, to be illusory. For how will we recognize any 'novel facts' predicted by the Project, when, and if, they arrive? There are no linguistic, — psycho — or socio — facts predicted by the team, as a result of which we can know that their hypotheses are proved correct. There are merely a few metaphysical statements about what is likely to happen in learning if the Project's hunches about language are taken up in practice. There are no widely available curriculum materials produced embodying the Project's ideas which can be tested out in the classroom. And above all, if the categories *are* able to be used, and teachers succeed in assigning their pupils' writings to them, how are these categories an improvement on others teachers have had for some time, or what do they have to offer that other — scientifically arrived-at — category systems, like, for instance, Jacobson's and M.A.K. Halliday's, do not have? Could they not, with their bias against the transactional, do *harm* in persuading teachers in say, science into using unsuitable and inappropriate forms of language and thus retarding, rather than encouraging, their pupils' development in science? Since no rational grounds are provided for the team's beliefs about language, how would we know they were *wrong* until it was too late? Since it is not, as I have found, an easy theory to analyse, it is not likely that teachers, failing to grasp its complexity, or failing to afford the expensive Research Volume, will seize hold of a diluted version of the theory which is dangerous and partial? I have already mentioned, in my introduction, the ironic fact that many teachers I have questioned who are trying to set up a 'Language across the Curriculum' policy understand it only vaguely as having 'something to do' with spelling or punctuation or 'speaking properly'.

Finally, how *relevant* is the system to teachers in the actual classroom, with all the complexity and flux that situation implies? Richard Pring, in a critique of Bernstein's classification and framing of knowledge, has much to say that is apposite here. Regarding Bernstein's theorizing about curriculum as 'an attempt to develop a theory of practice', he asks:

'How does this theoretical accou t relate to the complex practical reality in which teachers find themselves? How does the language of the new theoretical account relate to the language by which we ordinarily describe what is going on in schools? In what way can this be said to advance our knowledge of practical reality? In what way does this new theoretical account do better (in predicting or explaining) than what is normally done through the non-theoretical medium of everyday English . . . how does one distinguish between genuine theoretical development — new bodies of knowledge — and rather sophisticated theoretical games? How can one decide in this case whether the new "theory" is a genuine extension of our understanding of practical reality?' (Pring, 1975, p.62).

This has been my task in this chapter; to decide what sorts of theories *count* in educational research, what kind of theory the Writing Unit's theory is, and whether it contributes to our understanding of the problems it is theorizing about. I have concluded that it is a theory of such high generality that it is difficult to categorize, but that the central theory of language which *claims* to be scientific is not, because the status of its theoretical constructs is ambiguous, and its terms do not pick out any features in the scientific study ôf language, but are logically disparate in some cases, and imprecise, metaphorical and intuitional in others. As to whether it contributes to our understanding of curriculum reality, unless teachers are converted — ! use the word deliberately — to its views, the Project has merely cluttered the curriculum field with new stipulative definitions, the value of which, compared with what we have already, I have not found to be obvious. If they *are* converted, the theoretical framework will, as I hope I have shown, be damagingly restrictive, and will *distort* language in the process of making it fit these arbitrary models.

# Conclusion

From the foregoing chapters, it might appear that I am denying *any* usefulness to curriculum practice of the Writing Research Unit's work. This is not, however, the case. I have been concerned to evaluate it on its own terms — stated quite specifically — as *curriculum theory* and *curriculum research* and I believe I have demonstrated that as such it is not very helpful to practice. Neither could it, for epistemological reasons, provide the 'overarching theory of language' for schools that it aspires to, for I have shown that its approach to the languages of theoretical disciplines is deeply mistaken. For this reason, I do not believe that *any* 'overarching theory' of language is possible, and to seek to establish one is misguided. 'Language' can contain many theories; which one we choose depends on what we want to know about it, and there are many scientific, or philosophical/ethical, philosophical/descriptive, and philosophical/ aesthetic theories of language to match any particular set of problems or questions about language.

The usefulness or value of the Project lies *outside* its chosen field of operation, or at any rate outside the strictly defined bounds of theory and research. For those who can accept its position on language, it provides a powerful heuristic, provided that its statements are not interpreted too literally. It is right in some of its assertions about practice, even though they are based on intuitions rather than actual knowledge of classrooms; for instance, there *is* indeed too much dreary writing going on in schools, and teacher and taught seem trapped in a wearying vicious circle. Teachers often seem to feel that a lesson is not complete, or the children are somehow being allowed to 'get away with it' unless pupils are made to write something down 'before the bell goes'. I have seen many students destroy a good lesson, and all goodwill evaporate, because the interesting demonstration or discussion was brought to an end with an abrupt 'now write it down'. But I do not believe that the cause of the trouble is in the *kind* of writing, as the team do, but in the irrelevance of writing at *all* at such a point. I think we need *less*, not more, writing in schools, of *any* kind, even — or perhaps especially! — of the 'creative' kind; — 'don't *look* at it or Sir will make us write a poem about it!' — and teachers should justify every request they make for it on a rational basis. Since we learn to write in the various styles of the disciplines and art forms by internalizing models from our reading, copious *reading* in all subjects is clearly the priority in the early years of the secondary school, along with 'thinking aloud' in class with the peer group, *and* with the teacher as guide — 'a turning-around on what one knows', as Bruner puts it, in order to make sense of it: *metalinguistic* activity within the conceptual framework of *disciplined* inquiry.

Again, though the team are right to plead for more use of 'language in its art-like forms', it is wrong to do so in the framework of a curriculum project or theory, where it sounds a falsely prescriptive note, since we are not given any reasons to have more of such uses which make sense in an 'across the curriculum' perspective. But in a personal statement, like James Britton's *Language and Learning* the same pleas do make sense. And here I think we have the nub of the Project's failure; it is a *symposium* of ideas on language and language and learning — ideas from different personalities but who share certain convictions about language about which they feel strongly — masquerading as a Research Project. In their individual or joint books the members of the team are successful; but in the Writing Research Project, they have a different audience, not all of whom are accustomed to the high moral tone or intuitive subtleties of English teachers of their 'school', and who feel entitled to ask for evidence and reasons.

It is true to say, I think, that the ideas of the project make their appeal chiefly to English teachers (or perhaps, teachers in humanities) and principally teachers who favour the 'growth' or 'personal development' model. They are accustomed to 'expressive' or poetic uses of language having prominence; along with this view of their subject there often goes a dislike of the scientific or the useful. So, because they conduct *their* lessons mainly in the 'expressive', they are ready to see a wider role for it throughout the lessons of their colleagues; it might transform science into something they can understand and *like*. The personal note of the Project's writing makes its appeal here. Language full of 'I feel', 'I believe' — types of expression — the personal pronoun plus the emotional verb, — so prevalent in the writing of the Report, is the preferred mode of these teachers too. It is, for some unspecified reason, seen to be of more value than the passive voice or the objective statement. English teachers also, as I have pointed out, are used to regarding 'writing' as detachable from content in a way which does not happen in any other subject, except perhaps in that other symbolic system, mathematics. The idea of 'Writing across the Curriculum' does not puzzle them in the way that it perplexes other teachers. ('Writing *what* across the Curriculum?' I have been asked.)

But, if no 'overarching theory' is possible, what then? The answers to this question lie in two different directions, those for language teaching, and those for curriculum practice *as a whole*. To take the first-mentioned first, scientific or aesthetic theories of language, like those if M.A.K. Halliday, Jacobson, Susanne Langer, *et cetera*, can be useful in variety for solving particular problems in English teaching when they arise, or for illuminating insights into particular aspects of language. The teacher must be eclectic — no one theory will suffice, particularly since 'English' contains two disciplines, that of language and literature, and no theory has yet been concocted which, in proving explanatory for one, has not been less than just to the other. The teacher, however, must be informed about all these theories so that he can decide which are useful to his situation and make his selection. Then too he must become a language expert in *his own classroom*; not so that he can teach transformational grammar, but so that he can guide his pupils' explorations of language in as many different directions as possible. He should also attend to his own use of language, and if possible listen to himself critically, or get others to do so, for as Douglas Barnes (1971) has shown, we are not in general aware of the way in which our questions, replies, prompts, and so on determine the direction of the lesson and encourage or discourage pupils' efforts.

This last of course applies to all teachers, whatever their subject. And new techniques of 'discourse analysis', following on the work of Flanders, should help teachers to see themselves as part of a complex situation which is for them a research situation. And this brings me to the implications, for curriculum practice in general, of the failure of the large-scale curriculum research programme or theory to relate in any real terms to 'practical reality'. It seems now that such theories were starting at the wrong end; instead of *practice* identifying problems and *then* research being devised to solve them, the 'Grand Design' theories, as Hugh Sockett calls them, were devised *first* and then applied wholesale to practice. It is not surprising that they did not succeed in generating new hypotheses, or solving problems, since they did not take into account the teacher's perspective, or his complex practical reality, or his necessarily flexible approach to the problems of his situation. All this is true of the Writing Research Project; *teachers* were not asked, at the research stage, to identify problems; these were identified by the Research team. Nor was the practical situation of the classroom discussed with them; they were merely asked to collect data. Even here there was no contact. The report reveals as I have already mentioned, that the team knew *nothing* about the situations and personalities of the teachers who sent them scripts. They did not know the children either, and the practical classroom experience of the Project team members was long behind them. The gap between the practitioners and the theorists could hardly have been wider.

Fortunately, the paradigm of curriculum research is now changing.

The focus is on *action* research, and, although expert help can be called in, and relevant theory utilized, the practitioner is himself the reseacher. He decides what the problems are, in his own unique situation, and reflects upon what action to take. The problem of objectivity in this regard — how the teacher can be sure that his judgments are well-founded, — is being tackled by such projects as the University of East Anglia's 'Ford Teaching Project'. Sinclair and Coulthard's 'Discourse-analysis' project attempts something similar from a linguistic point of view. The problems are seen, therefore, to be much more complex than 'the need to develop writing abilities'. The language of the teacher, of the theoretical discipline, of the pupils, of pupil/teacher interaction, of the neighbourhood, — each is *an* important, but not the *only* important factor, and all these different aspects of language will come and go in prominence as the focus — the *practical situation,* — yields new problems for the teacher:

'Finally, it is necessary to respect the eclectic nature of curriculum studies. The focal point is the practical curriculum problem. To tackle this intelligently requires developing the arts of practice as well as mastering the complex way in which, through our language, we have come to conceptualize practical reality. But it also requires having a nose for those theoretical considerations which can be fed into the unique concrete, practical situation' (Pring, 1975).

Learning to write' or 'writing to learn'? It all depends; on who asks the question, and when, and where he asks it.

# BIBLIOGRAPHY

ALSTON, W.P. (1964) *Philosophy of Language*. Englewood Cliffs, N.J.: Prentice-Hall.

AUSTIN, J.L. (1962) *Sense and Sensibilia*. O.U.P.

BARNES, D. (1976) *From Communication to Curriculum*. Harmondsworth: Penguin.

BARNES, D., BRITTON, J., and ROSEN, H. (1971) *Language, the Learner and the School*. Harmondsworth: Penguin.

BERGER, P.L. and LUCKMANN, T. (1966) *The Social Construction of Reality*. Harmondsworth: Penguin.

BOYLE, D.G. (1971) *Language and Thinking in Human Development*. London: Hutchinson.

BRITTON, J. (Ed) (1963) *The Arts and Current Tendencies in Education*. London: Evans Bros.

BRITTON, J. (ed) (1967) *Talking and Writing in Education*. University of London Institute of Education.

BRITTON, J. (1970) *Language and Learning*. Harmondsworth: Penguin.

BRITTON, J. 'What's the Use?' In: WILKINSON (Ed), *The Context of Language*. *Educ. Review* **23**, 3.

BRITTON, J. *et al.* (1975) *The Development of Writing Abilities, 11-18*. London: Schools Council, Macmillan Education.

BRUNER, J.S. (1971) *Towards a Theory of Instruction*. Cambridge, Mass: Harvard.

BRUNER, J.S. (1975) *Entry into Early Language: a Spiral Curriculum*. University of Swansea.

BROUDY, H.S. (1972) *Enlightened Cherishing*. Urbana, Ill. : University of Illinois Press.

BULLOCK REPORT (1975) *A Language for Life*. London: HMSO.

BURGESS, T. *et al.* (1973) *Understanding Children Writing*. Harmondsworth: Penguin.

CAZDEN, C.B. (1972) *Child Language in Education*. New York: Holt, Rinehart and Winston.

COOPER, D.E. (1973) *Philosophy and the Nature of Language*. Longman.

DAVIES, A. (Ed) (1975) *Problems in Language and Learning*. Heinemann.

DIXON, J. (1975) *Growth through English*. Oxford.

EMIG, J. (1971) *The Composing Process of Twelfth Graders*. NCTE Research Report No. 13.

GUSDORF, G. (1975) *La Parole* (Speaking) trans. P. Brockelman. Chicago.

HABERMAS, J. (1971) *Towards a Theory of Communicative Competence*. Inquiry 4.

HALLIDAY, M.A.K. (1973) *Explorations in the Functions of Language*. London: Edward Arnold.

HALLIDAY, M.A.K. (1974) 'Language and Social Man', Schools Council Programme in Linguistics and English Teaching.

HARDING, D.W. (1937) 'The Role of the Onlooker', *Scrutiny*, VI, 3, 1937.

HARDING, D.W. (1962) 'Psychological Processes in the Reading of Fiction', *Brit. Journal of Aesthetics*, 11, 2, 1962.

HIRST, P.H. (1974) *Knowledge and the Curriculum*. London: Routledge and Kegan Paul.

HYMES, DELL (1968) 'The Ethnography of Speaking'. In: *FISHMAN, J. (Ed)*. *Readings in the Sociology of Language*. The Hague.

JOOS, M. (1961) *The Five Clocks*. New York: Harcourt, Brace.

JONES, A. and MULFORD, J. (Ed) (1971) *Children Using Language*. O.U.P.

KELLY, G. (1955) *The Psychology of Personal Constructs*. New York: Norton.

KUHN, T.S. (1970) *The Structure of Scientific Revolutions*. Chicago: University of Chicago Press.

LAKATOS, I. and MUSGRAVE, A.E. (Eds) (1970) *Criticism and the Growth of Knowledge*. Cambridge.

LANGER, S. (1960) *Philosophy in a New Key*. Cambridge, Mass: Harvard.

LANGFORD, G. and O'CONNOR, D.J. (1973) *New Essays in the Philosophy of Education*. London: Routledge and Kegan Paul.

LYONS, J. (1964) *Structural Semantics*. Oxford: Blackwell.

MARTIN, N. *et al.* (1975) *Understanding Children Talking*. Harmondsworth: Penguin.

MARTIN, N. *et al.* (1976) *Writing and Learning across the Curriculum*. Schools Council and Ward Lock.

MEAD, G.H. (1934) *Mind, Self and Society*. Chicago: University of Chicago Press.

MOFFETT, J. (1968) *Teaching the Universe of Discourse*. Boston: Houghton Mifflin.

O'CONNOR, D.J. (1957) *An Introduction to the Philosophy of Education*. London: Routledge and Kegan Paul.

OPEN UNIVERSITY (1972) *Language and Learning*. A Source Book. Routledge and Kegan Paul and the O.U. Press.

POLANYI, M. (1958) *Personal Knowledge*. Routledge and Kegan Paul.

POPPER, K.R. (1966) *The Open Society and Its Enemies*. Routledge and Kegan Paul.

POPPER, K.R. (1972) *The Logic of Scientific Discovery*. Hutchinson.

PRING, R. (1975) The Language of Curriculum Analysis. Doris Lee Lecture. ULIE.

ROSEN, C. and ROSEN, H. (1973) *The Language of Primary School Children*. Harmondsworth: Penguin.

SAPIR, E. (1961) *Culture, Language and Personality*. Berkeley, California: University of California Press.

SCHOOLS COUNCIL (1965) *English, A Programme for Research and Development*. Working Paper No. 3. London: HMSO.

SEARLE, JOHN. R. (1969) *Speech Acts*. Cambridge Univeristy Press.

SEARLE, J. (1972) 'Chomsky's Revolution in Linguistics', *New York Review Special Supplement*.

SEBEOK, T.A. (1960) *Style in Language*. Cambridge, Mass: MIT Press.

SINCLAIR, J. McH, and COULTHARD, R.M. (1975) *Towards an Analysis of Discourse*. Oxford University Press.

VYGOTSKY, L.S. (1962) *Thought and Language*. Cambridge, Mass: MIT Press.

WRITING ACROSS THE CURRICULUM PROJECT Discussion Pamphlets for Teachers. 1973-75.
From Information to Understanding.
Why Write?
From Talking to Writing
Writing in Science
Language and Learning in the Humanities.